Madness and Cinema

Also by Patrick Fuery:

Theories of Desire
Theory of Absence
Representation, Discourse and Desire (editor)
Cultural Studies and the New Humanities (with Nick Mansfield)
Cultural Studies and Critical Theory (with Nick Mansfield)
New Developments in Film Theory

Madness and Cinema

Psychoanalysis, Spectatorship and Culture

Patrick Fuery

First published 2004 by
PALGRAVE MACMILLAN
Houndmills, Basingstoke, Hampshire RG21 6XS and
175 Fifth Avenue, New York, N.Y. 10010
Companies and representatives throughout the world

PALGRAVE MACMILLAN is the global academic imprint of
the Palgrave Macmillan division of St. Martin's Press, LLC and of
Palgrave Macmillan Ltd, Macmillan® is a registered trademark in the
United States, United Kingdom and other countries. Palgrave is a
registered trademark in the European Union and other countries.

ISBN 0–333–94825–4 hardback
ISBN 0–333–94826–2 paperback

This book is printed on paper suitable for recycling and made from
fully managed and sustained forest sources.

A catalogue record for this book is available from the British Library.

Library of Congress Cataloging-in-Publication Data

Fuery, Patrick, 1957–
    Madness and cinema: psychoanalysis, spectatorship, and culture/
Patrick Fuery.
        p. cm.
Includes bibliographical references and index.
        ISBN 0–333–94825–4 (cloth)—ISBN 0–333–94826–2 (pbk.)
        1. Psychoanalysis and motion pictures. 2. Motion pictures—
Psychological aspects. I. Title.
        PN1995.9.P783 F84 2003
        791.43′01′9—dc21   2003051163

10   9   8   7   6   5   4   3   2   1
13 12 11 10 09 08 07 06 05 04

Typeset by Cambrian Typesetters, Frimley, Surrey
Printed in China

For Kelli – my light, my angel

Contents

List of Figures and Tables

Figures

Table

Acknowledgements

There is possibly something slightly worrying about finding one's name in the acknowledgements page for a book on madness – but all who feature here deserve mention for all the right reasons!

I wish to thank all the people at Palgrave Publishers who offered support and professionalism. In particular Catherine Gray, to whom I owe both an editorial and intellectual debt, and Jo Digby, for her constant (and always prompt) email replies that were filled with knowledge and good humour; Kate Wallis for so carefully watching over the end process; and Pauline Snelson whose copy editing allowed for a final polish. All of these people provided so much help from the conception to completion of this project.

I would also like to thank my colleagues in the Media Arts department, as well as other staff members, at Royal Holloway College. Collectively they have shown me tremendous support in some difficult and pressured times. I would especially like to thank Stella Bruzzi and Carol Lorac – who both offered so much kindness and friendship. I would also like to thank Horst Ruthrof for his intellectual challenges to some of my Lacanianisms, and for the warmth of his friendship. Thanks also go to James Donald for his encouragement and support as both a friend and colleague; and to Margaret Mills whose friendship goes back further than just about anyone else, and who continues to show me what it is to be a true friend.

And special thanks to Morgan because of all the delights he gives me; and for Noah who is our new treasure – for both of them there will always be my love. Finally, this book is dedicated to my beautiful wife, to whom I owe so much, for all that she gives me, and all that rests inside of her.

Preface

Socrates said that madness was preferable to 'sober sense' because 'madness comes from the Gods, whereas sober sense is merely human'; which seems to suggest that whatever madness is, its status and benefits or otherwise have been discussed for thousands of years. But more often than not these discussions and analysis struggle or collapse under the problems of defining what madness is. The idea behind this book is certainly neither to enter into the fray of defining madness, nor even look to its positive or negative attributes. If a book can have an origin (and it would seem that a book actually enmeshes many points of different origins) then the origin of this book was not madness but the spectator and meaning. Two motivations behind the book perhaps illustrate this best.

The first emerged from a desire to consider how meaning and knowledge operate in cinema, and in particular why some things seem meaningful and others do not, and how such a status changes across time or spectators. 'Meaningful' indicates a range of things here: why do we recall some elements of a film and not others (that is, do they seem more important or memorable because they are what is remembered)? Why do we notice a certain image that we had missed before (that is, something stands out now but on first viewing it was in effect invisible)? Why do we cry and laugh and recoil in fear from elements within a film (that is, why do we react as if there is an element of reality in films)? Why do some films seem to have 'greater' meaning than others (that is, why do we see meaning in some things and not others, how do certain films gain and keep such a status)? All of these seem to be questions revolving around the idea of meaning. The idea of knowledge is closely tied to this, and in order to make some sense of meaning we also need to understand how some things can come to stand as 'knowledge'.

In order to consider this idea of meaning and knowledge I chose to look at its other, madness. The strategy behind this was that any attempt to examine meaning always gets caught up in the very processes it is attempting to engage in. Madness is meaning and knowledge outside of themselves. Madness, then, is not a lack or absence of meaning, rather it is another version of meaning that for some reason or other has been placed in a special category of otherness. Similarly, madness is something that happens to knowledge, for madness produces a special type of knowledge. This is precisely what happens to cinema and its relationship to meaning. So, in these terms, madness and cinema share a certain position in terms of meaning. They actually allow us to take up a different position in order to work through issues of meaning and knowledge.

This leads to the second motivation. Cinema incites a certain position in order to exist. This book argues that we must take up madness in order to become a spectator, and only in doing so does cinema become possible. (Of course the same line of argument could be applied to the other arts, but cinema is the interest here). We have all experienced the effect of being in a large cinema, filled with a receptive audience. This is the film moment of hundreds of people as they are living out various emotions; their sorrow and happiness become tangible, their anguish and frustration palpable. Of course this is nothing new – the ancient Greeks spoke of theatre in this sense and there have been countless theories and accounts of such experiences – and there is nothing startling in observing how an audience (or individual) reacts to a film. But it seems, especially within this context of meaningfulness, that this socially sanctioned act of madness that everyone performs is an essential part of being a spectator. The idea, then, became to see if madness and the spectator could be used to think about cinema and meaning.

Is this a book about psychoanalytic theory and cinema? In some ways it is, but only in the sense that it would like to push the unfinished business of this coupling in another direction. And in some ways it is not, for it has at its heart this issue of how the spectator is formed through the insertion of a different type of knowledge – that is, the knowledge from madness. For this reason, this book is concerned with ideas that come from outside of the psychoanalytic field, whilst at the same time exploring some of the key issues and concepts from Freud and Lacan. Ultimately, however, it is a book that looks to the madness of knowledge and meaning through the eyes of the spectator as he and she enjoy the immensity of cinema.

CHAPTER 1

Madness and Cinematisation

Aren't you sometimes afraid of going mad? Judge Schreber

A certain type of contextualising

There are many ways to approach a topic such as cinema and madness, but the concerns here can be reduced to two – the operation of meaning and the construction of the spectator. We will come back to these in a moment, but for now it is important to acknowledge the context in which all of this will take place. In many ways the frame of reference for what follows is how we might use psychoanalysis in the understanding of cinema. Since the mid 1970s – with the influence of Metz's psychoanalytic approach to cinema, the publication of numerous articles in *Screen* exploring Freudian theory and film, and the rise of psychoanalytically-influenced feminist theory in the USA and UK – psychoanalytic approaches to cinema have played a key part in film studies. Furthermore, psychoanalysis has proved to be remarkably adaptable to other approaches (including feminism and gender studies, cultural theory, and so on) until we reach the current state of affairs where there are a broad number of critical approaches either directly or indirectly influenced by psychoanalytic theories. Part of the rationale for this book is to try and push these approaches further, not so much by engaging with them, but by developing a new line of interpretation.

Of course, what such historical developments have yielded is far from homogeneous and we must always be cautious of over-generalising. There is much disagreement and debate and a great deal of contestation in the theories of cinema and psychoanalysis. But this is always a good sign of ongoing thought. It is important to note that the fundamental approach here is to return to the primary texts of psychoanalysis – mostly Freud and Lacan – as well as two of the key thinkers of critical theory in recent times, Derrida and Foucault. Freud and Lacan legitimise themselves in any psychoanalytic study, so their presence here hardly needs defending. Derrida and Foucault are used for two reasons. They have both written major contributions on the underlying themes of this book (that of meaning and madness) and add different perspectives, thus avoiding some of the limitations of a 'straight' psychoanalytic approach. The second reason they are considered here is that they allow the development of this new approach to cinema to take place because they are both commentators on psychoanalysis itself. In other words, they work both with psychoanalytic concerns as well as outside of them. In this way, the aim here is not to simply conflate the four figures, or even to see them as necessarily sharing a common aim. Foucault and Derrida provide a sort of outsider's perspective to the central projects of Freud. Lacan, on the other hand, works as a key thinker of psychoanalysis, but is also a commentator on psychoanalysis. The self-reflexivity of Lacan, in this way, can be employed in a similar way to the framing ideas of Derrida and Foucault. Finally, all four thinkers demonstrate remarkably consistent desires to analyse knowledge and meaning, within and outside of their own areas of reference.

This 'return' to these four figures of critical theory is important for another reason. It would be wrong to think that all has been gleaned from their ideas, especially in terms of the analysis of cinema. There is still much work to be done in terms of developing a psychoanalytic approach to cinema, and its foundations reside in the primary texts. What is at stake here is to continue to test the validity of the ideas of Freud, Lacan, Foucault, and Derrida in terms of cinema. But what is of even greater significance is to develop a different sort of perspective on the operation of meaning in film, and the construction of the spectator. For it is in these two aspects of cinema that this book will argue that to be a spectator of a film is to experience madness; that this madness is a necessary requirement of watching all films.

This idea of the madness of the spectator is an attempt to advance current psychoanalytic approaches to cinema. This is why the book revisits the idea of the spectator and attempts to problematise its status and operation. The cinema spectator is seen here as a deeply unstable and tumultuous position, required to abandon the certainties of the everyday. As we shall note in a moment, the spectator is compared to the hysteric, neurotic, and psychotic in an attempt to witness the madness involved in watching a film. And, in the same way, meaning is also seen as an unstable process, constantly being formulated, broken down and resisted, only to be reformulated.

Sometimes it is easier, or clearer, to define something by what it is not, or by what it does not attempt to do, and in the spirit of that thought this book is not about the representation of madness in cinema. Certainly, this would have been a different task, and one with its own agendas and rewards. And there are moments in the book where the representation of madness will be taken up as a conceptual issue as well as to provide examples for the various points of discussion. However, what is ultimately at stake here is the issue of meaning; of how something comes to be seen as meaningful and something else as meaningless; and of how such categories can, under certain circumstances, seem to interchange with relative ease; and of how some meanings are more resistant to change than others. Within this agenda rests a whole range of questions, including: what are the devices that allow something to have meaning? How is the sense of meaningfulness established and sustained? What is it to contest meaning outside of itself? Who, within all the competing, interpretative voices gets to articulate meaning louder than anyone else? And which images, within the multiple sites of spectatorship, of a film seem to have and carry meaning more than others?

To address such questions, and the unending roll of others attached to them, this book has turned to meaning's opposite – madness. For, in the seeming collapse of meaning systems (such as is any form of language, including the visual), we find mirrors held aloft. Read any system that attempts to understand madness, to put understanding in madness – and psychoanalysis is the obvious one – and what we find is not a dismissal of 'this is madness and therefore meaningless', but rather that there is meaning of a different sort here. If madness is not meaninglessness, and instead offers a different *type* of meaning, then we come closer to understanding how anything can be seen as meaningful by looking at its opposite. If this seems like a dialectical approach, well perhaps in a Hegelian spirit of things it could be seen as such. Certainly Hegel's idea that things contain their own opposites within themselves, constantly finding themselves on the verge of sliding into their own other, is viable here. This is the dialectic of profound otherness, where what emerges as contrariety shares a commonality. Hegel's famous '[Life] wins its truth only when, in utter dismemberment, it finds itself' (Hegel 1977: 19) echoes this sentiment. Here, we look for how the sense of truth (as meaning) finds itself through the dismembering forces of madness.

This, then, is the first motivation for this book – the presiding of meaning through the upheaval of madness; the production of meaning in and through madness; and the sense that in madness there resides an otherness of meaning. There is a second motivation that is developed alongside this. This is the madness involved in becoming a spectator as we watch a film. Here we encounter a different set of problems. We are primarily concerned with the intersection of philosophical issues, psychoanalysis, and film theory in order to re-examine the formation and function of the cinematic spectator. This is the idea that the act of spectating is a form of madness. This will be worked at through three interpretative models – the spectator as neurotic, psychotic, and hysteric. Before we outline these ideas a note should be made of the overall structure of the book.

Some notes on the structure of the book

In the language of art there is a type of painting that consists of three panels – the triptych – with a series of companion images running underneath called the *predella* (often this depicted the lives of the saints). There is a sense of the triptych here, with the two 'side' panel chapters – *Representing the Impossible* and *The Limits to Knowledge* – taking up issues central to the cinema apparatus[1] and its relationship to madness. The first of these two chapters will look at the impossibility of representing madness. Such impossibility comes to be seen as a necessary attribute of madness; in other words, for it to be madness, there is an almost necessary resistance to any form of representation. Part of this is when the impossible itself is seen as madness. The chapter will also consider how cinema has utilised aspects, stories, and images from the extraordinarily long history of madness, which includes all its discourses, to form its own representational processes. In this way, cinema can be seen as part of a continuation of the stories of madness, both retaining the past and inventing its own representational forms. Finally, the chapter will argue that an inherent and necessary

attribute of all forms of madness (particularly in the ways of representation) is resistance. Madness thus comes to be seen as consti-
tuting all those sites of resistance and impossibility. Madness
subsumes its own representational and interpretative difficulties so
they become part of the overall process. Madness is what cannot be
done.

The Limits to Knowledge, the other side to this triptych, will offer
another aspect to this quality of resistance. For here we witness no
less than the ways in which both madness and cinema contest and
produce knowledge. We arrive at this not simply as a comparative
statement (that madness and cinema do similar things to contest
the idea of knowledge), but that there is a certain madness in
cinema's potential beyond knowledge. *Cinema,* in these terms, is
more than its film texts – it is a relational process of knowledge and
meaning produced through the formation of the spectator. Just as
madness can be seen as knowledge's other and a site of resistance,
so cinema can present us with other knowledges, becoming a resistance to meaning through them. How we get to such a position is
the third image in this triptych – the central panel (to continue the
analogy). This is what is termed here the *becoming spectator.*

We deploy this term *becoming spectator* to indicate that there is a
continuous, unsettling, perhaps even disjointed, process that
cinema invites. This is not the complacent spectator of pleasure (to
parallel Barthes' idea of the reader) but a spectating position
caught up in resistance, impossibilities, and at the limits of knowledge so that the only comparable position to it is madness. How
much we would want to liken this to a sort of implied spectator (via
phenomenology[2]) is open for discussion. This is avoided here
because what is at stake are the processes of becoming a spectator,
as it follows that madness requires madness. To argue for a site that
can be prescribed as such would seem to go against the spirit of
what is being posited here. The site of madness and the spectator
is perhaps just as impossible to articulate as madness itself is. If
there is a *predella* to this triptych, it is the lives of the spectator in
the turbulent contexts of neurosis, psychosis, and hysteria.

It is important to note that these three types of madness are
used to explore relationships between the spectator and the film.
This includes a range of issues that are relevant to madness, the
site of spectatorship, and cinema itself. A significant part of this
includes the moments of blurring between reality and fantasy, and
the issues of created world orders and the structure of the real;

transgression, ethics and beauty as the cinema spectator challenges, and is forced to challenge, systems of moral positioning
and desire; the textual structuring of cinema that allows it to
construct madness out of a vast range of images and sources, at the
same time participating in them and operating outside of them.
How we can come to utilise such specific and identifiable terms
(from the discourse of psychoanalysis) will be taken up in a
moment.

The *predella*, then, is not about distancing madness, but about
aligning cinema – one of the dominant forms of textuality of our
times – with it. This is to suggest that it is only through a version of
madness that being a cinematic spectator is at all possible. The
idea here is that cinema demands a certain commitment, and the
spectator undertakes a certain relationship to the film, that can be
read as a type of madness. Without madness cinema would not
make sense, could never be seen as meaningful or having knowledge. We, as spectators – the neurotic, psychotic, hysteric spectator
– can only make sense of cinema through the madness that over-
takes us at the time of watching the film, of recalling its moments,
reacting to its narratives, and thinking/talking about it to others.
Let us take this up within the context of a statement from Lacan as
he challenges the analysts in his audience with the following
thought:

> Don't we analysts know that the normal subject is essentially someone
> who is placed in the position of not taking the greater part of his inter-
> nal discourse seriously? Observe the number of things in normal
> subjects, including yourselves, that it's truly your fundamental occupa-
> tion not to take seriously. The principal difference between you and
> the insane is perhaps nothing other than this. And this is why for many,
> even without their acknowledging it, the insane embody what we would
> be led to if we began to take things seriously. So let us, without too great
> a fear, take our subject seriously.

(Lacan 1993: 123–4)

To place this quote in some context will allow it even greater
power.

Schreber, a psychotic that we shall have reason to visit throughout this study, asks his analysts *'Aren't you sometimes afraid of going
mad?'*[3] – and it is to this that Lacan offers the strategy and neces-
sity outlined above. Schreber's question has relevance not just to
his analyst, all psychoanalysts, but also for everyone. (Why such a

question continues to be posited in terms of fear will be taken up later). The only difference between the insane and everyone else rests in this attitude towards madness and knowledge. But of course this is an enormous repository, filled with almost unimaginable images, convoluted histories, and always with an air of compulsion. To take cinema seriously is not just to work up the analytic side of things; becoming a spectator involves taking what is being seen on the screen seriously, that is, as if it is something real, something meaningful. This necessarily includes the literal sense of this – that cinema is a subject of seriousness – and a more abstract version. The latter being the idea that when we become spectators of cinema there is something beyond the interplay between reality and pretence. There is something that dissolves the distinction between film and what could be called the everyday existence of reality. Such dissolution becomes part of what we see as madness. In this complex idea about the relationships between reality, the cinematic text, and the spectator we discover one of the fundamentals of cinema as a textual process. For cinema, the text is not simply that which is projected and watched, it must also include cultural positioning, the act of spectating, the relationship to other sign systems, and judgements of a range of things including aesthetics, ethics, and ideologies. This is the issue of what cinema is in terms of its ontologies, its different types of existence.

Ontology is crucial to madness because, along with meaning/knowledge, it forms part of the definitional act. Our concerns with madness and cinema channel the definitions of madness towards the formation of the spectator. At various times a sense (and it can only ever really be a sense because of that resistance to representation that madness contains) of a definition of what madness can be will be offered within this context. This includes issues of reality, resistance, power, knowledge, meaning, and ethics. There is always, however, the spectre of a madness that can never be defined, for this is precisely what constitutes its role in the order of things. In this, we witness madness' capacity to disrupt through its absences and lacks. So, madness is a form of reasoning that lacks the systems of, say, logic; it is a form of desire that lacks the boundaries of cultural restraint and propriety; it is a construction of subjectivity that works on absences (the denial of the speech of madness, such as the hysteric, or of an inability to order causality in the paranoid, and so on); and it is the text that resists through absenting formal constructions normally seen or expected such as beginnings, middles and ends in narrative, or the idea of a dominating, single voice that offers a single story. Because of so much resistance and impossibility, the work of madness becomes the work of absence.

The impossibility of madness

Foucault titles the 'Appendix' to his work on madness *Histoire de la folie à l'âge classique* (1972) as *'Mon corps, ce papier, ce feu et la folie, l'absence d'œuvre'*. The first part (My Body, This Paper, This Fire) is, of course, a reference to Descartes and the issues of madness and the reasoning for its exclusion from western thought. This was Foucault's reply to Derrida's comments on *Histoire de la folie à l'âge classique* (*Madness and Civilisation*), taking up the key idea that reason excludes madness in any pursuit of truth – that it is, as Foucault puts it, disqualified. This is derived in no small part from Descartes' assertion that the utterances of the mad are to be excluded from his philosophical method. It is significant that the second part of Foucault's appendix refers to madness as the absence of an œuvre.[4] This is about the impossibility of representing madness (or giving it its own voice) through any of the discourses that are created around it and for it (including, for example, the arts, psychoanalysis, and religion).

In this sense madness isn't anything, but everything has the possibility of madness. The spaces of madness are impossible to specify and so seem to be everywhere. It is this potentiality that has fuelled, through the centuries, reactions of awe, respect, fear, moments of seduction and intimidation, exclusion, religious mania, as well as scientifications such as the medicalisation of madness. The absence of the work of madness means that the acts and signs of madness are always seen through filters of different systems. Psychoanalysis, medicine, the arts, religion, morality – these are what gives the absences tangibility. Yet, they must always remain other to madness itself.

This is why cinema loves madness, and, it is argued here, why the cinematic spectator is always watching from the shadow of madness. What, then, is it to cinematise madness? By this we mean not simply the representation of madness, the images and narratives that continue the line of showing us the literal, cultural models of madness. Rather to cinematise madness is to allocate a space for madness within the formation of cinema itself, to note the ways in which cinema, its spectators, and its function within the world order, operate through madness, to note the attempts to create a work where only absence can reside. To remain true to the idea that madness is about absences, we note that to cinematise madness is not to create presences (for example, the representation of the mad in a film) but to follow the lacks of desire, meaning/knowledge, and subjectivity as they form part of cinema. In following these lines of madness the cinematic spectator regains the possibility of contesting.

In a lecture on madness, Foucault argues that the opportunity to contest (his concern is with the social order in general) has been lost in the contemporary age.[5] For Foucault, this is tied up with the relationship of knowledge and madness, and it is what motivates much of his thinking. Foucault wanted to trace the process so he could investigate social institutions. Elsewhere he states: 'Thus, in order for the big centres of internment to be opened at the end of the seventeenth century, it was necessary that a certain knowledge of madness be opposed to nonmadness, of order to disorder, and it's this knowledge that I wanted to investigate' (Foucault 2000: 261–2). Part of the argument here is that becoming a spectator of cinema – and recall that this does not simply mean just watching films, but of taking things seriously – is one of the ways the populace has continued the contesting of reason and order through a type of madness. This becomes part of cinema's seductive qualities. The other point of investigation is what sorts of knowledges are produced by, and through cinema and its spectators.

Questions abound in such an assertion. Let us take up two of the more obvious ones. Firstly, why is it that we do not feel mad when watching a film? Such a question originates from the discourse of medicine that has dominated the definition of madness since the mid part of the eighteenth century. It assumes that madness is of that order defined through and by the medical, and that it is these discourses that have the capacity to recognise and define it. Where, such a question implies/demands, are the medical versions of madness in the spectator? Yet madness must surely be beyond this – and the 'beyondness' of it will cover far more than what the discourse of medicine ascribes to madness. At the very least, madness must include the discourses of medicine, and all the others that have been a part of its long history. And, significantly, madness must also include all the resistances, ruptures, defiances, to such discursive practices.

Madness is at one level what medicine determines it to be – but it is also constituted of the vast narratives that lie beyond medicine, some of which will run counter to it. So to look towards a site of spectating that can be called neurotic or psychotic, for example, is in part to borrow the terminology of one discourse, and at the same moment exceed that discourse (of medicine, of psychoanalysis). And because madness has always been seen as formulated on absence, as excluded, as otherness, it will always exceed any of the dominant discourses, the grand narratives, of the time. Madness is excess, and one of the most significant aspects of this is to be in excess of what attempts to define it.

Of course, the next question that might be asked through such a line of investigation is why use psychoanalysis in this study when madness is beyond it? The answer is twofold. Firstly, psychoanalysis, for all its faults and incompletions, represents the radical other to every attempt to engage with madness (which necessarily includes those attempts to exclude it). To echo both Foucault and Derrida[6], we must do justice to Freud for allowing this new sense of madness that exists within us all, including our culture. Psychoanalysis may not provide all the answers to madness, but it does offer the possibility of dialogue. Part of this agenda is to acknowledge that psychoanalysis is a continuation of many lines of western thinking that precede it. In this sense, it is part of a much broader philosophical investigation – and this is directly useful for our concerns here. The second reason we engage with psychoanalysis here is to participate in the continuing development of film theory that draws on these ideas and issues. In this sense, the discussions that follow are also concerned with how psychoanalytic theory might be expanded beyond the uses so far (such as the theorising of the gaze and scopophilia, phallocentric viewing positions, feminist versions of psychoanalytic theories, the psychosocial ideas, as well as the more literal attempts to use psychoanalytic concepts in the study of the humanities). And so madness becomes the (theoretical) centrepiece of psychoanalysis and cinema as well as the site of spectatorship.

Exceeding all attempts to define, represent or even record it, madness is placed in a position of mutability. Here, what defines madness is not its signifiers, but rather its effects. To absent, to exceed, to resist – all of these are what constitutes madness. And it is these same qualities that will allow us to position cinema within the discourses of madness. The interplay between the film and the spectator will often produce complacency, simple pleasures, cultural conformity, presences, containment, and ludic joy. Yet, there are also those moments of *jouissance*, of spectorial resistances, of film exceeding itself and its cultural production.[7] In short, there are those moments within the cinematic apparatus where madness exists. We call this madness here because this is not the replication of what medicine calls madness, or what philosophy attempts to analyse in its systems of knowledge; rather this is part of the culmination of the impossibility of madness as it appears in countless forms and manifestations.

This leads us to the second part of such a question: Is it really possible to take up systems of madness and equate them to the act of watching a film? To offer some answer to this, it is important to realise that, as we have noted above, another underlying issue of this book is to reconfigure some of the relationships between psychoanalytic theory and cinema. In this way, 'systems of madness' designates those ideas that have been developed to make madness present, to give it visibility. Psychoanalysis is part of the discourse of madness, and not just the attempt to speak to it or allow it to be spoken. Similarly, cinema is part of the discourse of madness, not in its representations of madness, but what it requires of the spectator to exist and operate – which is part of taking cinema seriously. In adopting such a position we are avoiding the idea that if cinema and madness are of the same order, then psychoanalysis can be employed in the interpretation of both of them. As tempting as such a line is, what is being posited here is the idea that madness, psychoanalysis, and cinema have a *sui generis* relationship. And, for such a relationship to exist, there needs to be a particular type of subjectivity taken up – that of the spectator. In becoming a spectator we allow the possibility of madness and cinema.

In using psychoanalysis, by exploring and utilising its terms and themes, its narratives and case histories, we run the very real risk of making this a psychoanalytic reading of cinema. And in some ways this does take place here, and it is indeed part of the objective. The risk just mentioned, however, is the separation of analytic methodology, psychoanalysis, and its object, cinema. This would be to see them as heading in different directions, but the concern here is what they share. And so madness haunts the other two, testing and challenging, placing continual demands on psychoanalysis' capacity to interpret, and cinema's potential to disturb, unsettle, and to be turbulent – in and for itself, and in and for the spectator.

Here we come up against the phenomenon of cinema as a site of potential madness, but a potential that is not always realised. More often than not we will only glimpse this madness in cinema and its spectators, and this is the dis-ease of cinema to which the cure is pleasure, the realisation transgression. This language of transgression is something that is a constant struggle: the struggle to allow it to exist, to realise it, to perhaps simply acknowledge it. Of course, to demarcate something like madness and cinema through transgression does not give us any greater purchase on the issue of definition. To 'replace' the impossibility of madness with the unrealised transgression does not give us a definition, but it does edge towards a strategy. Foucault's sense of transgression (via Bataille) is interesting in this regard:

> Transgression is an action that involves the limit, that narrow zone of a line where it displays a flash of its passage, but perhaps also its entire trajectory, even its origin; it is likely that transgression has its entire space in the line it crosses. The play of limits and transgression seems to be regulated by a simple obstinacy: transgression incessantly crosses and recrosses a line that closes up behind it in a wave of extremely short duration, and thus it is made to return once more right to the horizon of the uncrossable.
>
> (Foucault 2000: 73)

So it is with cinema and madness. The line they are forced to cross and recross is, it is argued here, the same line. And the agent of these crossings, the one who is forced to return to the horizon (of cinema as a social and textual order, of sanctioned positions, of the limits to knowledge, of making sense of things) is the spectator. Cinema, like madness, offers the possibility of transgression to the spectator. There are no guarantees here, no certainties of any line being crossed, no surety that the spectator will resist and risk pleasure in order to gain transgression. All exists *in potentia* – and sometimes that is exactly enough. For this is the potential of madness in cinema, it is the cinematisation of madness.

CHAPTER 2

Representing the Impossible

How does one represent that which cannot by it very nature be represented, that which constantly resists translation, interpretation, and stability? The impossibilities of defining madness are also part of the impossibilities of representing it. And yet the images and discourses of madness in its various forms of representation have always been a part of culture, and they surround us in ways that have never happened before. For madness is never a single moment, a composed paradigm that remains fixed. Instead it is an accumulation of discourses whose boundaries are impossible to map. Foucault's point that part of the discursive formations of madness in the twentieth century has been its medicalisation, for example, demonstrates just how impossible a task it is to show madness in itself. There has always been a mediating set of discourses (medicine, the textualising of it as painting, literature, music, and so on, animality, the supernatural, religion, the law and its systems of arbitration, and so on) so that we experience madness through something. So much so that whenever madness is shown it has arrived beyond itself already.

The two orders of representing madness then become either the reconfigured madness (sexuality as mad, possession as mad, excess as mad, vapours and bile of madness, madness as it breaks the law or threatens the ethical order) or that which is othered as madness (other cultures, other meanings, other sensibilities, other representational systems). This chimerical attribute of madness works across these two orders – either there is something within the sign that makes it seem mad, or something cannot be explained, located within the established order, and so is designated as madness. Either way, madness becomes a site of exclusion and impossibility – excluded from the rational, known world, and impossible to figure because of this. And it is this, this resistance and impossibility, that madness does so well. This is what lies not at the heart of madness (how can we ever know that without risking madness) but at the skin. We do not penetrate madness to see its impossibilities; we experience them as we rub up against it. It is this initial site of resistance that shows us we are witnessing madness. It is a site that has become so invested with fear that the systems for representing it often carry a sense of the medusal – to gaze directly at madness will bring about a transformation of the self. But doesn't everyone really want to catch at least a glimpse of such an extraordinary face?

And so there is a compulsion to represent madness, to reveal its signs and show its workings. Part of this is derived from the very nature of the impossible, for when madness is represented (no matter how inadequately, or how over-simplified), impossibility itself is touched on. If it were possible to represent madness then all those other things that are seen as beyond the representational field (such as ecstatic pleasure, freedom, impossibility itself) may also come into focus. Cinema has become a repository for the discourses and images of madness that have developed over thousands of years. In its relatively short history, cinema has effectively absorbed, conventionalised, and established the representations of madness for itself as a textual practice and for the wider social domain. In this way, cinema has become one of the primary producers of representations of madness. And in such representational processes we also observe interpretation, negation, exclusion, and creativity. In some ways, cinema's representational fields have been innovative in this regard, producing images that are unique to its qualities; in other ways, cinema has borrowed heavily from social conventions, other art forms, other historicising systems, and other discourses (such as medicine, philosophy, and psychoanalysis). In this sense cinema has become a dominant representational mode of madness. However, it has also become part of the discourses of madness that, significantly, were being produced out of medicine, notably with the birth of psychoanalysis.

Our interest in these images of madness as they emerge out of the discourses are threefold: firstly, to consider how cinema draws on a number of established ideas and forms of madness from different sources; secondly, to consider the types of resistances that madness brings with it to any form of representation; finally, how the excesses of madness always challenge the systems of representation, and therefore of meaning itself. These are large subjects to deal with, and often we shall have to indicate rather than analyse in depth. Still, the idea that what we are dealing with is a certain impossibility (the impossibility of representing madness outside of madness) will tend to unify such schematics.

Representation: cultural paranoia, wanderers, and social transgression

Representation itself is never simple, and rarely transparent. It is the process of carrying over, of placing within a frame and rendering a difference. The representational processes are more often than not kept hidden, for differing reasons, but to the same effect. When we are confronted with something as resistant to representation as madness surely is, these very systems of representation are often both foregrounded and challenged. For madness is the antithesis of representation and always contains within itself a core of resistance. This, of course, is the issue that drives part of the debate between Foucault and Derrida – how is it possible to contemplate madness through a rationality that must, by definition, exclude it?[8] Part of the reason why representation is never straightforward is that any sign that passes through the system of representation is immediately transformed by the repressions and exclusions, considerations of representability, notions of meaningfulness, forces of conformity, specifics and traditions of the medium, and so on.

The representational processes of cinema construct a certain type of sign in order that narratives can develop and the spectator can make sense of the structures – this much is obvious. The issue here is when that which is being represented in cinema – images of madness – challenges the processes of cinematic representation, and consequently cinema itself. This partly explains why cinema (and it is not unique in this although it does have certain idiosyncratic and specific properties) relies on other sources to represent madness. The patterns of images and narratives already established make the processes of representing the impossible more possible, or at least more viewable, more aligned with the conventions of representation. A recurring difficulty with this is that the complexities give way to simplifications and normalisations, often to the point that what is excluded is precisely what is essential. The danger then becomes one of formulaic representations of madness that really only function because they have historical precedents. To understand better how cinema both reinforces such representations and sometimes challenges them, the ensuing discussion will take up some of the dominant images of madness and look to their historical and textual sources. The issue at hand is a much broader one, however. Contained within the ways cinema has developed images of madness are the issues of meaning, authority, power, the contesting of truth, and the function of otherness. This is true not just of the cinematic apparatus, but the position of cinema within the other discourses dealing with madness, including law, medicine, and psychoanalysis. Cinema is thus part of the larger order that does not just represent it, but also formulates madness beyond itself.

One of the key issues here – and it is a recurring one for this book – is how we differentiate between the literal representation of madness in cinema, and the ways in which themes and conceptualisations of madness can be used in the analysis of cinema. What is at stake in such a distinction is the ways in which madness can be conjoined with cinema and what the territory between the two looks like. In doing so, we move from issues of representing madness (which hold no real interest to this particular work) to utilising madness to understand cinema. This may seem like a curious strategy – employing madness as an analytic process, using unreason to construct reasoning. Here, we have madness held like a mirror to all that attempts to exclude it, position it as the other to reason and analytic coherence. Part of the motivation behind this – and it is one that drives much of the discussions throughout this book – is the idea that cinema is closer to madness than may first appear. What such an approach highlights is the multiplicity of madness as a discourse. Already we have three distinct versions of representing madness within this discourse: madness as it is seen to be showing itself; madness as it is figured through other discourses, such as cinema and psychoanalysis; madness as a source for interpretation. From this, we argue that it is the totality of these – and others – that constitutes madness, and not just the acts and images of madness that are presented through the representational, textualising fields of the arts or the filtering, interpretative discourses of the sciences. From this point on, *madness* here must include all these variations, as well as others that will emerge as we proceed. For most of the book, we shall be primarily concerned with how madness can be seen, in its multitude of guises, as an analytic process for cinema; however, it is also important to recognise the relationship between this idea and the other forms of madness (its representations and its acts). To this end, what follows are some aspects of concern on the representation of madness in cinema.

Because we are not simply dealing with the representation of madness in film, what constitutes the field of study here is something beyond such depictions. It is not enough to look to those films that show acts of madness – the crazy, insane figures, the demented acts, the popularised versions of paranoia and hysteria, or even the white-coated psychoanalysts. This is because, in part, although there are many films that engage in such representations, ultimately such a study will lead to a simplifying arrangement of the categorising of types and overt manifestations. This is the idea that cinematic representations of madness can be seen as some sort of cultural and historical insight. One particular aspect of such representations, however, does concern us. This is those moments when the representational boundaries are blurred.

Films that represent madness – that is, those that participate in the long history (certainly one that commences from the Middle Ages in Europe[9]) of stories of madness – are diverse in themselves, and there are many examples of cinema's attempt to narrativise madness. Such films are significant in their role in textualising madness, of placing it within a cultural and historical context, of making it part of the current social order and consciousness (note, for example, the representation of the serial killer as madness in the 1980s and 1990s of Hollywood, or madness and drug culture – both pro and anti – of the 1960s in Britain and the USA). This much is obvious, and a different study could usefully trace the relationship of the representation of madness to cultural events and attitudes. In doing so, it would provide a sense of how certain moments in a culture's history change and are reflected in the depiction of madness. One of the reasons why madness is particularly effective in such a study is that it is located, almost by definition, on the fault-line between meaning and all the challenges to meaning. Madness risks meaning in order to be heard; it is the hinge between established ways of thinking and their radical other. It is the copula between what is understood and the possibilities beyond understanding. Locate this spot within a cultural history and one finds the self-reflexive moment unhindered, or, possibly, a foregrounding of the repressive systems that attempt to sustain the fear of the Other.[10]

Such representations of madness become the literal struggle with showing things that do not rest easily in the signifying practices. In these terms, cinema becomes the liminal site between madness and reason. In such unsettling moments, when we experience not simply the representation of madness, but the disjunctive force that the unrepresentable carries with it, here all possibilities abound. In his address on representation, Derrida concludes with the following: 'But perhaps the law itself manages to do no more than transgress the figure of all possible representation. Which is difficult to conceive, as it is difficult to conceive anything at all beyond representation, but commits us perhaps to thinking altogether differently' (Derrida 1994: 34). This is the possibility that madness with cinema, in that cupola between what is and what could be, has – the chance to think altogether differently.

But to return to a point that intimates such a possibility rather than manifests it. A straightforward example of this type of study of representations and cultural contexts (and one that is of least concern to us here except, perhaps, to show the travails of representing madness) would be the examination of cultural paranoia in science-fiction films in 1950s' Hollywood. Here we see a relatively overt correlation between a socio-political and socio-psychical moment (the US fear of Communism) and a textual manifestation (through metaphor) of it. There are at least three levels at which this version of madness could be approached. The first is the sense of madness attributed to the invading ideology. Consider *Invasion of the Body Snatchers* (Siegel 1956) with the wild-eyed doctor who is initially treated as mad, or the automaton doubles whose oddness makes them eerie and unsettling in much the same way that madness is often depicted. This is ideological difference as madness as those who do not share the ideology of 1950s' USA are shown as not human. Compare this to the representation of individual paranoia, such as Harry Caul in *The Conversation* (Coppola 1974). Here the paranoia becomes an isolating, disempowering process of a single person, while in *Invasion of the Body Snatchers* it is originally posited as survival (be wary, watch others) and only much later can such films be read within the sense of isolation, this time culturally. The second version we see in these 1950s' films is a form of madness at the social level. The most direct manifestation of this was the genuine fears of invasion by the American populace at the time. When this became so entrenched in the national psyche it operated as cultural paranoia, allowing it to be transferred into political policy. The third is the fear of the madness itself (the fear of the irrationality caused by the other two). This type of representation of madness has a long history, for it can be linked to any depiction of another culture that is defined by the eccentric, the frenzied, even the uncultivated.[11] One of its most direct historical links is to the twin forces of the eighteenth century's sense of the civilised order against the cultures of Otherness, and the colonisation ideologies of the nineteenth century. Cultural paranoia acknowledges the need to colonise the unconscious in order to control, and represents the fear of this. A key to the processes of ideological power in these terms is the ascribing of madness to difference.

A different sort of example is the representation of the wandering, displaced outsider as a sign of madness. Films of this type would include a diverse range, such as *The Cabinet of Dr Caligari* (Wiene 1920), *The Night of the Hunter* (Laughton 1955), *Taxi Driver* (Scorsese 1976), and *Betty Blue* (Beineix 1986). These are the signs that operate as madness because they come to represent the existence outside the stabilising/stable realm of the cultural ideal of the family and its social structure. Their emergence into the social order (that which comes to stand for the norm, the sane, the rational) is seen as a disjunction, and only once they are dispelled can stability (of the family order, of mental calm, of eased fears) be restored. Such images of madness are drawn from ideas that became concretised in the nineteenth century. The centrality of the bourgeois, patriarchal family to the social order of this period was directly linked to the prevention and/or cures for madness. The family, it was argued, prevented mental instability (particularly hysteria), and when it broke down, madness ensued. (We shall return to these issues later). This is also part of the intervention of the other into structures that are considered part of the social order of things, such as the family, morality and ethics, cultural practices, and social spaces. In the examples listed above, this would include the disruptive forces of sexuality and passion (with Betty's erotic-charged intervention in Zorg's life in *Betty Blue*); the cultural outsider (a type of *Stultifera Navis*, this time depicted as the travelling carnival of Caligari that disturbs the city spaces); perversions of religion and childhood (such as the scission of the family in *The Night of the Hunter* caused, initially, by the absent father); and the psychosis of morality (in Travis Bickle's version of the world in *Taxi Driver*). In a certain way these are signs of hysteria – the madness that is located (historically) as outside the family, and can be 'cured' through the assertion of familial structures.[12]

Another example of these sorts of literal representations of madness would be the flows and rushes of excess and transgression in certain types of characters. Films such as these are more often than not marked by a structure of parallel and mirroring. That is, the idea of excess works because contained within the film is a mirroring point that shows what excess is not or what it is that is being exceeded. Similarly, transgression is seen from a point that is marked within the textual world order. Thus, transgression can only take place once this point is breached, even if within other contexts any number of moments and actions could be seen as transgressive. Even if most such demarcations take place within a larger cultural order, the fact that there is an internal mechanism to the film that is needed to mark such excesses and transgressions means that inventiveness is often necessary. Similarly, a film can set up degrees of transgression, marked by this point. For example, Mark Lewis, the central character in *Peeping Tom* (Powell 1960), is seen to be acting with excess and in a transgressive manner, and therefore his actions are interpreted as mad, because the narrative locates a point of recognisable and acceptable sexuality (the family, monogamy) and anything beyond this is excess. What now must seem as mild acts of sexuality (the photographing of women in states of undress, but certainly never naked) are positioned in the film as part of the larger moments of excess and transgression of Lewis. As such, they become aligned with the murders – it is as if his acts of murder are understandable or have meaning (that is, can be interpreted and be made sense of) because he performs these other, minor acts of excess. In being positioned in this way they also become part of the most extreme versions, which is the photographing of women at the moment of their death, notably by a camera that both films and murders at the same moment. So the madness is not simply contained within the murders (and the way they are carried out) but through every single action and minor divergence of Lewis.

Madness is seen as something that pervades all acts and thoughts of the mad, and everything they do is a point of confirmation for this. This is the economy of madness, for everything that is performed can be taken as transgression. In the moments of seeming non-mad there is a sense of hyper-normality, so that the everyday moments of the mad are madness. To continue the example further, the photographed death in *Blow Up* (Antonioni 1966) becomes linked to obsession, compulsion, alienation, and loss of meaning (all related early on, through this economic process, to a dismissal of the ethical and lack of commitment). In short, it stands for the disintegration of reason, perhaps symbolised most overtly by the tracking camera at the end of the film as it bounces to follow a tennis ball that isn't there. This is a transgression and excess not just of the mime group or Thomas, the photographer, but also of the filmic apparatus itself. The camera movement of following the non-existent ball invites the spectator to participate in the madness. (This is something quite common to the films of Antonioni – consider the wandering camera shots in *The Passenger* (1975) which capture the spectator's gaze with alienating dispersal of the shot that contains its own meaning).

In a different way to *Blow Up*, the version of the photographed death in *Strange Days* (Bigelow 1995) shows how the point of transgression marks the madness beyond the ethical. It is only the serial killer's acts of 'filming' the deaths that seem transgressive, and not the (admittedly more minor) transgressions of other characters (such as drug taking, street violence, illegal dealings in software). It is interesting, although beyond our direct concerns here, that all these examples develop a connection between technology and the acts of madness. In *Peeping Tom* it is the murderous camera, in *Blow Up* it is the camera (both his own and the camera of the cinematography) that mediates death and alienation for Thomas, and in *Strange Days* it is the computer technology that allows the recording of memories and seen events.

A final example (type might be a better term for there is also considerable diversity here) of the literal, overt representation of madness in cinema is the transgression of social orders that leads to mad acts. As with the other form of transgression, what is clearly marked within the film (and it is heavily drawn from the cultural context) is a point that confirms what acts are to be seen as madness through transgression. This would include things such as the centrality of the family and monogamy. *Fatal Attraction* (Lyne 1987), for example, has the forgivable, and therefore sane, transgression of the male (Dan Gallagher) as distinct from the mad, excessive transgression of the female, Alex Forrest.

In a different, but not altogether unrelated, way gender roles have also been used to show madness. The sexually active women in film *noir* can be seen as a version of hysteria, whereas similar acts of sexual promiscuity by men are assertions of masculinity. In this way, male sexuality confirms the socially acceptable and rational, female sexuality confirms women's susceptibility to madness through their physiology. The history of this can be traced directly to the attitude towards hysteria, as well as nineteenth-century attitudes towards women and reading. Women's physical make-up, it was argued, made them unable to resist temptation, more easily seduced into madness and passion.[13] In some ways, the serial killer Buffalo Bill in *Silence of the Lambs* (Demme 1991) is not that far removed from such sensibilities. His desires show the transgression of gender as both cause and effect of madness, but it is always held up that it is his desires that drive his acts. This idea of transgression is not just sexually derived. Films that show a disruption to an economic balance through greed, such as the character of Gordon Gecko in *Wall Street* (Stone 1987), or the overstepping of established lines of business (no matter how immoral such lines may be) in *The Godfather* (Coppola 1972), have a taint of madness to them. This is a version of madness derived from the excess rather than the actual acts themselves. We have not mentioned films that actually specify madness within the psychiatric institution – such as *One Flew Over the Cuckoo's Nest* (Forman 1975) and *Girl, Interrupted* (Mangold 1999) – we shall let these stand as examples of an order of films that position madness as its subject matter.

To such specific examples, and even 'types', we can add an almost countless list of films that have attempted to represent madness, which of course will include the categories that form the material for psychoanalysis (such as paranoia, schizophrenia, neurosis, hysteria, and so on). These are all the films that show madness within the representational types that cinema has established for itself and inherited from other sources, and cover the full generic range from the comic to the tragic, and cinematic forms from documentary to narrative. These are the figures of madness in cinema – from the *dementia praecox* in *Fight Club* (Fincher 1999) to the obsessional neurosis in *Mad Max* (Miller 1979), or, from a different perspective, *Morgan: A Suitable Case for Treatment* (Reisz 1966); from the hysteria in *Betty Blue* to the megalomania in *White Heat* (Walsh 1949). Such films will include the mad love of the French New Wave (from Godard's *A bout de souffle* (1960) to Truffaut's *L'Histoire d'Adèle H* (1974)), the torments in Polanski's films (the darkly comic of *Cul-de-sac* (1966) to the darkly fearsome in *The Tenant* (1976) and *Repulsion* (1965), the sexual-psychical convolutions of *Last Tango in Paris* (Bertolucci 1972) or *Man of Flowers* (Paul Cox 1983). These, and so many more. Such figures of the mad will be familiar in part because they are held within cinema's own inventions of the mad, and in part because they belong to the long traditions of the representation of the mad. This is reinforced further through western culture's centuries-old practice of using intertextuality in the representation of the mad. In other words, we see in the representation of madness a recurring set of images that return to one another.

So, cinema utilises the figures of the mad, referring to the established images and stories, which in turn have always been self-referential. Interestingly, Foucault sees this (he is speaking more broadly of the textualisation of things) as part of the coherency of representing madness:

> In its various forms – plastic or literary – this experience of madness seems extremely coherent. Painting and text constantly refer to one another – commentary here and illustration there. We find the same theme of the *Narrentanz* over and over in popular festivals, in theatrical performances, in engravings and woodcuts. . . It is likely that in Bosch's *Temptation of Saint Anthony* in Lisbon, many of the fantastic fauna which invade the canvas are borrowed from traditional masks; some perhaps are transferred from the *Malleus maleficarum.*
>
> (Foucault 1987: 17)

To this we add cinema, for it has become part of this very tradition of intertextual referencing, and it continues the same sorts of images. This is why we find images of the *Malleus maleficarum* (the 'instruction' book of the Spanish Inquisition on how to torture the body to free it of evil spirits) in so many serial killer films; why the images of entrapment by the mad are so heavily coded, more often than not from the dank and fetid cells and underground pits of the eighteenth and nineteenth centuries.

Just as Foucault sees the *Narrentanz* repeated throughout cultural representations and enactments, we can find it in the cinema of Polanski, Cronenberg, Greenaway, or Kubrick. The cinematic function of such intertextual references (either within films, or across to the textual traditions of representating madness in literature, drama, festivals, paintings, and so on) is that it provides an immediately recognisable discourse of madness, and so becomes a readable version of the unrepresentable. The depiction of madness through the eyes, for example, flows from paintings (from the more overt images found in Goya, Brueghel, perhaps even Rubens to the religious mania/devotion in Crivelli's Saints) to cinema in the haunted eyes of Caligari, Nosferatu, Jack in *The Shining* (Kubrick 1980), Aaron Stampler/Roy in *Primal Fear* (Hoblit 1996). The other function of this intertextuality is to contain madness, to provide a border for its excesses, to 'translate' its sense of the unknowable. The recurring images of madness function as a discourse of power, attempting to control something that is, by definition, beyond such control.

This is cinema's participation in the discourse of madness from the perspective of the rational, derived from a historical tradition. It is the representation of madness through paradigms that have been articulated outside of madness, and so cannot be described as actual madness. Even something like the Surrealist and Dadaist attempts to create a mad cinema fail at this level because they must necessarily commence from the Symbolic (that is, Lacan's version of the cultural order) and continue to borrow from it. *Un chien andalou* (Buñuel/Dali 1929) is not madness, but rather a film that attempts to recreate an experience of madness, or at least a sense of the madness of the unconscious; Cocteau's *Le sang d'un poète* (1930) reminds us of a dream, but will always have more structure than a dream is capable of. Just as *Psycho* (1960) can be said to be about (a popularised version of) psychoses and childhood trauma rather than being an actual depiction of madness; or *Pi* (Aronofsky 1998), no matter how much it attempts to unsettle narrative formula and spectating positions, is a representation of madness.[14] Beyond these deliberate attempts to depict madness, replicate it, simulate the experience of it, is the narrative process that indicates madness in order to withdraw from it. In many such films madness is rarely evoked, but it is allowed to exist as a shadowy presence, a path that may explain through dismissal ('this is all but madness'), yet one that the narrative chooses not to take up. Thomas Anderson/Neo in *The Matrix* (Wachowski Bros. 1999) is offered madness as a possible solution to what is taking place, but the narrative, spectator and, eventually, Neo does not, nor cannot take this up. Similarly, *Rosemary's Baby* (Polanski 1968) continually offers the two possibilities of possession and hysteria. This shadowy double of madness does not negate madness, but it turns from it in order to construct a different sort of repository of ideas and images.

But once we move from such a relatively obvious set of examples, where madness is the theme, to another set of examples where it is less apparent, the representational field becomes more problematic. There are a large group of films that may not appear to fall into this category of films about madness, but could still be interpreted within such a frame. Many of the actions of Ethan Edwards in *The Searchers* (Ford 1956) can be read as madness in part because of the nature of his deeds (obsession, violence, mania – there is even a sense of the schizothymic within both character and narrative) and in part because it is a disturbance to the cultural icon of John Wayne. Yet, this is a film that is not readily categorised as one representing madness, even with its theme of the obsessive drive for revenge and the (psychical) recouping of John Wayne as Western (and American) hero (albeit as confirmed outsider). In these terms, how far removed is this from many of the slasher films of the 1980s and 1990s? These films may hint at the madness of the killers, but more often it is the themes of revenge, sexual transgression, and (occasionally) the supernatural that define the narrative and explicate the events. Yet, the acts are also located within a cultural order that would have been seen as madness. To this type we would also add the comic. Here, the acts of madness are read through the generic operations of humour and rather than questioning the sanity/rationality of them they are seen as functioning in a different manner.

All of these examples – the transgressive, the obsessive, the supernatural, and the comic – present us with a range of films that are not readily categorised as ones about madness because the madness within them has been transformed into something else (such as Rabelasian humour of excess and parody, sexual drives, revenge). To reconfigure them as being about madness is not particularly difficult, but it does shift the representational processes, and thus also how we read and interpret them. To say that the acts and speech of the Marx Brothers are mad is quite different from saying they are funny, even given the psychopathologies of humour allowed by Freud in *Jokes and Their Relation to the Unconscious* (1983) (or even, and why not, the sorts of differences made by Hegel between the comical and the laughable). And to say Ethan Edwards is mad is to present him in a light that makes his actions less noble in part because they lose their sense of purpose and design – indeed they would lose their sense altogether. The return of the daughter to the family must then be seen as an almost accidental moment in an ongoing madness. It thus becomes something more like Travis Bickle's returning of Iris to her family in *Taxi Driver* – an unintentional consequence of unrelated acts driven by types of madness. Thus madness can be transformed to appear otherwise, but the madness is still about.

What we are presented with, then, is a larger order of things. From these two broad types – the films that use madness as a (narrative) theme, and the films that could be interpreted as having madness in them – we can see some of the difficulties and impossibilities of prescribing madness as a type of generic order. Instead, we will pursue a different sort of approach – the idea that madness can be used in the analysis of cinema itself, both as an apparatus (and by this we mean the broad sweep of the processes of narrative, filmic technique, relationship(s) to reality, the cultural/historical and ideological positionings of cinema, the formation and actions of the spectator, and so on) and the individual films themselves. Before proceeding with this, it is necessary to engage further in the relationships between madness and cinema, not so much as an issue of representing madness but of the sense of madness itself as it exists alongside cinema. This *alongside cinema* is to consider how madness and cinema can be seen as having similar, or even the same, attributes; it is also to position the two within certain cultural, textual, and interpretative contexts. The heterogeneity of cinema (which must include all films, all genres, all versions of narrative, documentary, and so on) defies all attempts to reduce it to a singularity, and this is not what we mean to say when we position madness and cinema alongside one another. However, the concern here is with how we might map out the discursive practices of the two within these contexts of culture, the text, spectatorship, and interpretation. This will be the issue at hand now, in a preliminary fashion, and the overall theme of this book.

Cinema alongside madness

To ask either the question 'what is cinema?' or 'what is madness?' will send us off in directions that are without end or are complete dead-ends. At one level, the major points of interest when we speak of the alongsideness of cinema and madness are their relationship to knowledge, meaning, understanding, interpretation – in short the pursuit of some sense-making process. If we put to one side the complexities of meaning (for example, what can an image of madness mean beyond that it is/comes to stand for madness? Can meaning be ascribed to acts of madness? Where does the sense of meaning originate in madness? Once we attribute a specific meaning to an act of madness is it still madness? How do we understand something like madness? (These are issues that will be taken up later). The underlying relationship of knowledge, meaning, and understanding to madness is one of schism. Madness is what it is because it is outside of knowledge, challenges knowledge, functions as knowledge's Other, and so on. This would include the binarism of reason/madness, and knowledge and its collapse. This is the way in which madness is excluded and disallowed from the realm of reason.

At the same time, this schism provides not a total separation of madness and knowledge, rather it sustains the sense of mutual definition. This is why we earlier described madness as forming a cupola. Madness is defined here not as lacking knowledge or being meaningless, but of having an order of meaning and knowledge within itself. If anything, madness is seen as more meaningful than those signs traditionally ascribed as meaningful. How can such a contradiction operate? In part, this has come about because the frame of madness rarifies the sign in its otherness to knowledge and meaning. The mad act is seen not as lacking meaning, but of having a meaning that is obscured, or different, or contested, or simply unresolved/unresolvable. In this way, the signs of madness are the absolute version of *différance* as meaning is acknowledged, but is premised on a fundamental sense of difference and is in constant deferment. This, in turn, becomes one of the defining aspects of madness – it is the sign that declares itself as meaning otherwise. Furthermore, part of this status is that meaning contains a plurality within madness that appears to be in a constant state of multiplying. These meanings of madness are thus in a state of flux, and any attempt to understand them must take into account not only what they might signify, but also what they are capable of transforming into. An essential feature of madness (which is also the representation of madness) is this capacity to resist interpretation through a seemingly endless generation of meanings. Reading madness is haunted by such fecundations.

This aspect of madness and its relationship to knowledge will continue to be an issue throughout the ensuing discussions. The declaring/demanding nature of meaning in madness is part of its seduction. We pursue the images of madness because of this promise, even if there may well be continual deferral, misunderstandings, and thwarted attempts at resolution. The idea, for example, that any act of madness has a meaning underlying it propels so much of the narrative in cinema. Obsession, passion, excesses, extremes and exaggerations of emotions (including fear, loneliness, love), as well as the discourses and materiality of psychoanalysis (such as psychosis, hysteria, schizophrenia), form much of cinema's material; and within these narratives the search for understanding mirrors the cultural sense of madness. What is at stake is not the sense of a lack of meaning, but of understanding signifying practices that are more meaningful because of their attachment to something like madness. Madness, the moments that are designated as beyond understanding, thus become the ways of understanding. It is the exaggerations, the otherness, of signs filtered through madness that makes them more transparent. It is as if the mad sign, the sign twisted and exalted, performs a type of eidetic reduction, where things are seen in terms of their essence. Thus, mad love is love in extreme, obsession is a purified version of the less ordinary existence in life, paranoia becomes vision with greater clarity. A specific example of the representation of this relationship between madness and meaning/interpretation, that of the serial killer films, will help illustrate this.[15]

When the sequence of murders takes place in a film about a serial killer, the spectator, like the investigators (the police, detectives, scientists, or even the innocent passers-by), immediately looks for a meaning located within the acts of madness. A great deal of the cinematic energy (including the narrative structures, filming processes, uses of sound, close-ups, repetitions of sequences, and so on) is directed precisely at creating a sense of meaningfulness in the acts. The crimes become highly motivated signifiers, part of a code structure that needs to be understood and read. The killings become carefully constructed messages – sometimes to the law, sometimes to the self-reflexive killer, but always to the spectator. What may be articulated by the uninformed voice in the film (that necessary site whose position serves to strengthen the sense of meaning behind the acts) as randomness in the killings, and therefore beyond comprehension, is subsequently shown to be full of very precise and methodical meanings that can, and often are, traced back to a moment in the past. This aspect of the serial killer films reflects a sense of madness found in what Foucault describes as the great fear in the eighteenth and nineteenth centuries, where knowledge and complexity are seen as potentially dangerous: 'The more abstract or complex knowledge becomes, the greater the risk of madness' (Foucault 1987: 217). It is this fear that contributed so much to the formation of mental asylums and the confinement of madness to socially organised sites of restraint. This became one of the defining forces in distinguishing madness and reason in western thought. Cinema thus becomes both, and at the same moment, a part of the asylum and a force against it. Cinema continued the line that madness is something to be observed (both for pleasure and also as a form of preventing sane people falling into madness).

The solution to these obscured meanings behind the killings and crimes, however, must come from a very specific source, usually the empathetic individual defined by their initial (and often continuing) state of bewilderment. More often than not, what is essential for the solving of the riddles and enigmas is not the rational efforts of science, but the emotive. Compare the representation of surveillance technology in a film as early as *White Heat* to any number of films that appeared in the 1990s on the hunt for insane criminals (such as *Silence of the Lambs, Se7en* (Fincher 1995), *The Bone Collector* (Noyce 1999)) and what they have in common is the inadequacies of technology to solve the puzzles and capture the insane without the help of emotion, often depicted as a sort of perverse empathy. No matter how sophisticated the rational, logical procedure might be, the vital part of the solution more often than not lies in the revelation of a combination of some element from the past (that is, personal history), a creative or idiosyncratic approach, and a highly individualised system of thought. These very qualities and attributes of the mad acts are seen as part of the killer's mind as well as that of the solver of the puzzle (the detective as psychoanalyst). Even when the meaning is pursued by the figure of the psychoanalyst, as in *Spellbound* (Hitchcock 1945), it is through the emotive (in this case love) rather than the purely analytic that finally allows sense to be made of the events. In all these cases, both the disturbed and the analyst are positioned outside of the normalising moment of the social and historical order. What allows all of this to take place is that there is a persistent force that declares all acts of madness to be attached to some sense of meaning. The smallest detail, the most insignificant of acts, the slightest fluctuation of the body, become filled with absolute signification, or at least having such potential. What they mean is in constant doubt (until the final revelations), but that they mean something is never questioned within the discourse itself.

This example of the bond of signification between the serial killer and his/her others, which includes the person who solves the crimes as well as the spectator, is part of a much larger order of madness, and can be traced back to the origins of western culture's sense of madness. For it is not just about the relationship of madness to meaning and knowledge, it is also about how madness is always framed within the sense of humanity. This, for Foucault, marks one of the earliest formations of madness:

> In this delusive attachment to himself, man generates his madness like a mirage. The symbol of madness will henceforth be that mirror which, without reflecting anything real, will secretly offer the man who observes himself in it the dream of his own presumption. Madness deals not so much with truth and the world, as with man and whatever truth about himself he is able to perceive.
>
> (Foucault 1987: 27)[16]

This may be why the mirror is such an integral part of the representation of madness, and why so many of these images draw on the aspect of reflexivity. This can be the literal representation as well as more symbolic variants.[17] In these mirrorings, the attachment of madness to subjectivity is strengthened. Not only do we see meaning in madness – which is both the sense that there is something meaningful in madness as well as the idea that when we look to madness we begin to understand something about the nature of meaning – we also see ourselves. This makes the images of madness in cinema both ones of narcissism and epistemophilia – we desire knowledge and we desire ourselves in the images of madness. When these two are conflated, as so often is the case in the representation of madness, one of the implications is that there is knowledge of the self to be found in the images of madness.

There is another variant on these themes of knowledge and reflexivity, and this is one that stems from the almost obsessive drive for rationality in the eighteenth century. One of the consequences of this drive was to formulate a sense that (European) rational thought embodied humanity and anything outside of that was less, a supplement, a copy or weak imitation. Madness came to be seen as part of bestiality, and so excluded from human reason.

This is in contrast to the idea that madness contains knowledge and insight denied to the rational mind. It is noteworthy that cinematic representations can allow for both depictions (madness as reducing the mad person to a bestial state, or madness as illumination), but true to a long textual tradition, one is usually excluded in order for the other to exist.

To continue with the serial killer example, the meaningful plans of the carefully executed madness of Hannibal Lecter (whose capacity to understand the works of other people's psyches is presented in tones of admiration), in *Silence of the Lambs*, or John Doe (the serial killer who enacts his murders with great ingenuity), in *Se7en*, are positioned in contrast to the animality of the other mad people (such as Multiple Miggs in the neighbouring cell to Lecter) and the unrestrained act of revenge killing of John Doe by David Mills. Mills' lapse into unreason/animality through the violent act of vengeance at the end of the film is at the cost of his humanity. These dual representations allow the pre-classical sentiment of madness as meaning (and even as insightful) to exist alongside the classical age's insistence on the bestial nature (and therefore outside reason) of madness, as long as they are somehow made distinct. Within individual films, we can find extremes of models of historical attitudes towards madness: the eighteenth century's ideas of the bestial and the immoral nature of madness sit beside the sense of its divination from the Renaissance in *Se7en*; Betty's hysteria in *Betty Blue* at various times shows elements of the uterine explanation from the Greeks[18], of the humours, effect on the body from the seventeenth century, of the need for marriage and the weakness of women towards mental instability from the nineteenth century, as well as an affinity to the sort of women's sexuality as power found in some feminist readings of Freud's Dora.[19]

The prestige of the image: the transpositionality of madness

The representation of madness in cinema can thus be described as transpositional. By this, we mean that the representations draw freely on the full historical and cultural range of discourses on the mad, which are then transposed into the narratives of cinema itself. It is this inmixing of representations and explanations that dominates cinema's images of madness. This is more than merely

the locating of different images and ideas of madness within a
single text, however. The cinematic transpositionality of madness
includes the cultural lineage of the representations of madness,
but also includes the other aspects of madness we have noted
earlier – that of its relationship to systems of meaning and understanding, and the cupola effect of cinema to madness and reason.
Madness in cinema is more often about a multitude of historical
ideas and images than the fixing of a single moment. This partly
explains why so many of the representations found in film are
historically anomalous and even anachronistic. The dank and fetid
cells of mad people from the eighteenth and nineteenth centuries,
for example, still dominate the images of institutions in cinema set
in recent times.

A consequence of this is that the relationship of cinema's
images of madness to knowledge and meaning are often formulated within a diverse and heterogeneous composition of sources,
including its own rule-governing processes. In this way the representation of madness in cinema approaches a status beyond itself.
The very nature of their transpositionality means that these
moments show an essential aspect of western culture's attitude
towards madness. Such is the unknowable facet of madness that
attempts to represent it are compelled to draw on the expanding
images of mad acts as they have been constructed. Compare this,
for example, to a comment by Foucault on the position of madness
in western thought (he is referring to the eighteenth century in
particular, but it has remarkable resonance for the case of
cinema): 'The ultimate language of madness is that of reason, but
the language of reason enveloped in the prestige of the image,
limited to the locus of appearance which the image defies. It
forms, outside the totality of images and the universality of
discourse, an abusive, singular organization whose insistent quality
constitutes madness' (Foucault 1987: 95). Here we can see not
simply cinema's processes of representation (the prestige of the
image), but a key feature of cinema's function in the discourses of
madness, meaning, and knowledge. As with madness, cinema's
abusive, singular organisation is its capacity to resist the universalising of discourse; it continually presents us with challenges to the
totality of images. This is the other significant aspect of madness
and cinema. By considering something that continually resists
representation we potentially gain insight into the systems of
representation.

Another feature of cinema's transpositionality and madness is the relationship of the image to morality. Madness has often been presented as a type of beyond to the moral structures of the social order. As such, it cannot be judged by them, and yet is constantly positioned as a threat to them. This relationship to the moral order is fairly constant within a signifying practice notable for its transitions and variations. Within cinema's representations, the challenge to moral orders through madness is to be found in the full range – from the supernatural to the criminal, from the comic to the melodramatic. Part of this relationship is what has been noted earlier – one of mirroring and self-reflexivity. The acts of madness mirror and distort the moral order, and in doing so operate within a site outside of morality itself. Similarly, the moral order sets up the perimeters for defining what constitutes madness by defining itself as precisely not that. Here, transgression through morality becomes part of the signifying practice of madness. Furthermore, we often find a curious dialectic between morality and madness that may initially appear as a system of causality, but any attempts to articulate a teleology usually present many unresolvable issues. This is the relationship of morality as a cause of the madness (for example, *Breaking the Waves* (von Trier 1996), *Psycho*, and *Sister, My Sister* (Meckler 1994)) as an inversion of the idea that madness is a challenge to the moral order. The oppressive moral order is positioned as causal, or the acts of madness are seen as the reason for such moral rigour to prevent such madness.

The interplay is significant in that it demonstrates the transpositions of madness within cinema. These may be defined generically. For example, film *noir* and the gangster films of the 1940s through to Penn's *Bonnie and Clyde* (Penn 1967) present transgressions of the moral order as excessive (read mad) and therefore punishable. In this sense, the conventions of the genre attribute a certain relationship between the madness of death and sexuality (in terms of drives) and the breaking of the moral codes. In this way, the genre itself comes to define how the spectator reads actions and characters in terms of madness. Yet, of course these conventions allow for their own rule breaking, and the neo-*noir* cinema such as *The Last Seduction* (Dahl 1994) and *Bound* (Wachowski Bros. 1999) plays with the madness of the moral order. By drawing on the established conventions of the genre (and part of this includes the issue of morality) neo-*noir* films allow for the questioning of patriarchy and heterosexuality as normalising practices. Women with active desires are not figured as mad, although they can still be seen as excessive. Similarly, *Oh Brother Where Art Thou?* (Coen Bros. 2000) inserts a madness into the 'classical' gangster genre (a form that could be said to end with *Bonnie and Clyde*). *Oh Brother Where Art Thou?* takes the style and form of the escapee film, inserting images that threaten madness (the flood scene, the river siren scene, the Klu Klux Klan scene, even the speech of Ulysses Everett McGill, and so on), only to be held in check by the parodic. As with madness, this is one of cinema's most compelling attributes, as it shows the capacity to resist and even transgress the moral order without necessarily adopting responsibility for the actions.

Here, we can adapt the historical dimension of the 'scandal of unreason' and witness how cinema has adopted a type of heteroglossia in its relationship to, and representation of, madness.[20] For all the sorts of relationships of madness to its others (reason, Law, sanity, conservatism, and so on) developed throughout the history of western thought – animal–rational, unreason–reason, the Fall–divinity, non-meaning–meaning, immoral–moral, spectacle–spectator, and so on – cinema continually draws on the images and narratives of madness without a need to historicise, categorise, or fashion a name for them. Madness in cinema can be defined precisely as this inmixing of types across the full range of historical and cultural models. Two of the reasons why this can work is that cinema is the art form born in the age of psychoanalysis, and cinema is particularly good at blending different cultural forms. The Freudian age contributes to cinema's transpositional constructions of madness, whilst its textual affluence (that is, the rich diversity of cinema and its capacity to represent an extraordinarily wide range) allows these different forms to be held together.

Animality, passion and fear

If this idea of transpositionality and heteroglossia as cinema's inmixing of versions and readings of madness can be seen as one of the key defining attributes of madness in film, then we can note further some of the significant motifs in such representations. Mention has already been made of some of these, but a few more examples will help illustrate the ideas; it will also enable us to track some of the historical moments in the formation of images of madness. The examples to be considered are animality, passion, and fear. Once we have these we can move towards the other key issue at hand – the essential feature of resistances to any form of representing madness.

Animality

As we have noted above, in the eighteenth and part of the nineteenth centuries, western thought developed the idea that madness reduced the individual (or even group/culture) to an animal-like state, and subsequently was seen as being directly related to the negation of rationality. The loss of reason was seen as a loss of civilisation, of culture, of the features that the age of Enlightenment defined as humanity (and so took the mad away from God) – and it was this that constituted the greatest threat of madness for this time. For, in this, madness became part of a religious destruction (which in itself is linked to the Middle Ages and the idea that madness was part of witchcraft and the work of the devil). Such conceptualisations of madness can be seen as part of the larger order of the discourses of this time, including the formation of certain types of sciences (including medicine), the rise of Eurocentrism and policies of colonialism, the developments of Rationalism and Epiricism (such as is seen in the ideas of Locke and Hume). In other words, the constructions and definitions of madness directly reflected the ways in which Europe ordered its world, including the defining of knowledge and reason.

A significant part of this was to define a Eurocentric view of the world, and position civilization as a key. Part of this was the division of the (European-defined) civilised and the inhuman other. As Foucault puts it: 'For classicism, madness in its ultimate form is man in immediate relation to his animality, without other reference, without any recourse' (Foucault 1987: 74). It is not difficult to see how such a social and intellectual climate would be antagonistic to madness and the irrational, and to all that was seen as other to Europe. For example, Rousseau's concepts of the social contract and the idea of the General Will rely on a foundation of group cooperation and the intervention of a supposedly rational, organised government apparatus. As such, there is no space for what is perceived as the irrationality and antisocial attributes of madness. It is not just at the level of the social that we see such attitudes; knowledge became something to be upheld and valued in itself (beyond the question of whether or not it was 'good' knowledge). The *Encyclopédie* of Diderot and D'Alembert attempted to categorise all knowledge and put on display the achievements of the 'age of reason'. Such a collection necessarily positions knowledge and madness as not simply antithetical, but also as mutually exclusive. Knowledge – specifically the rational (reason) – was seen as necessary for the formulation of morality and the movement towards God. Madness, on the other hand, denied morality and thwarted the humanities' elevation.

From such a social and political environment madness was seen as that which undid the achievements of the rational mind. The dominant characteristic of madness became that of the bestial. We have already noted some cinematic examples of this – the animality of certain types of killers is one. Visually, the mad as animal have a number of common signifiers in films – disheveled hair, ragged clothing, dirty, stooped, bestial gait, wild eyes that seem more animal than human. They are prone to outbursts of grunts and screams instead of speech; their actions are unpredictable, explosive and rapid. They have little or no control over bodily fluids: James Cole, in *Twelve Monkeys* (Gilliam 1995), crouches and dribbles in the scene where he is visually interrogated as insane; Max Cady sweats profusely in *Cape Fear* (Scorsese 1991). The version of madness from the age of Enlightenment formulated the animality in a very specific way, not of nature but of danger: 'Madness in the classical period . . . is rooted in the threats of bestiality – a bestiality completely dominated by predatory and murderous instincts' (Foucault 1987: 193). Jack, in *The Shining*, becomes more bestial as his madness (possession?) progresses – and it is a form of madness that is entirely directed towards the murderous and away from the cultured sensibilities of writing, care for property (a property related to financial enterprise), and care for the family. In the scene where Jack's wife, Wendy, discovers his writing is nothing but a repetition of 'All work and no play makes Jack a dull boy' Jack physically moves from the cultured and rational to the bestial. Nature itself, through the symbolic use of (natural) light through the windows is seen as unhinged as the bestial is asserted and murderous madness takes over. Speech moves from the rational and seemingly calming ('I'm not going to hurt you. . .') to the violent ('I'm just going to bash your brains out') within single sentences. This entire scene, from Wendy, shot so strangely (extremely low shots) as she reads the manuscript, to the knocking unconscious of Jack at the top of the stairs, holds the two extremes of the rational and madness. But not, significantly, as opposites, but as two forces bound together. This is the inflection given the mad as animality from the postmodern age. It is the impossibility of schism as each part clings to the other, for part of this madness is precisely this doubling, enfolding, of madness and the rational, animality and the cultured.

And as with many of these types of signs, if the mad are signified through animal-like qualities, the inverse can also be established with cultural difference coming to stand for a referent of madness. The representations of Native Americans in classical Hollywood Westerns are often shown as more animal-like than the European-influenced soldiers. Subsequently, their culture and actions become positioned as the irrational and potentially mad. Similarly, the ugly in *The Good, the Bad, and the Ugly* (Leone 1966) is the least European-looking (that trait belongs to Clint Eastwood's 'Blondie'), most animal-like and also the one most irrational, most mad-like. Of course, the irony here is that these films by Leone are Europeanised Westerns, a sort of exaggerated mirroring of the canonised Western. This is the distorted mirroring of culture, often infused with the religious. The non-Christian culture becomes one of madness that is reflected in the culturalised image of European Christianity opposed to the animality of the non-Christian cultures of, for example, Orientalism.[21] The other version of this, typified in the Leone Westerns but disseminated throughout a much wider array of films, is the core of European cultures deemed most rational as opposed to the 'outer' cultures (such as Eastern Europe, Southern Spain and Italy) of excess. Hence the vampires out of the East, passionate, wild-eyed Hispanics, and so on. Almodovar taps into such stereotypes of madness to construct his characters as ones immersed in a post-Franco frenzy of sex and mental disturbances.

Another variation of this animality is the suicidal mad person whose madness positions them outside of the rational social order. Briggs in the *Lethal Weapon* (Donner 1987) series, Max in the *Mad Max* series, Nikita in *La Femme Nikita* (Besson 1990) all demonstrate acts of madness and animality which makes them outsiders to the socialised world. And just as part of the technique for handling madness in the eighteenth century was to try and educate it[22], so we see in films of this type the socialising of the mad by the highly rational partner or institution. The function of

Roger Murtaugh in the *Lethal Weapon* series is to illustrate the madness of Briggs by contrasting his actions with his own rationality, to socialise him by reintroducing (that is, educating) the system of inter-relations (largely through the normalising force of the family), and to re-humanise him by negating the death drive. This is precisely what happens through the sequence of films, until in the final parts there are fewer suicidal, insane and antisocial qualities and actions that define the character in the first place. Briggs starts out as a Hamlet figure, and his actual madness is always in question anyway. So the loss of the loved one (the wife/Ophelia/the Father) may have caused madness, or may have given the reason for feigned madness.

Another feature of the eighteenth century's theorising and treatment of madness (and its animality) relates to the Eurocentrism of thought. Rousseau's famous idea of humanity being the centre, and Europe being the centre of that centre, excludes so much as a supplement. Furthermore, for Rousseau, these supplements where also typified as lack and evil. The evil of the mad in their animal qualities is a recurring motif of the times. Madness was located as outside and threatening to the rational world order, a force that could disturb and even destroy the good of the world. We find cinematic versions of this in many forms: science gone wrong – making the rational scientist animal-like, such as Dr. Frankenstein, Dr. Jekyll and the father/scientist in *Eyes Without a Face* (Franju 1959); attempts to rule/destroy the world such as in *Fifth Element* (Besson 1997) and *Twelve Monkeys*; even the threat of madness from the outer parts of Europe (the castles and mountains of Eastern Europe for the vampiric figures as well as werewolves) to the perceived civilised world. Even if such figures are not seen as mad (although most of them do exhibit qualities of madness) contact with them often results in madness. And it is the movement away from the centre that gives the madness this quality of animality.

Passion

The weight of textual examples (from all forms of the arts) between madness and passion makes this relationship somewhat apparent; and because it is a relationship so strongly forged in culture it is one we will return to often. For this brief section all that is needed is an indication of the sorts of (historical) factors that have influenced some of the cinematic representations of madness and passion. For this reason, we shall keep to a relatively focused example of productivity and its relationship to madness and passion. Following from the previous discussion, we can note that one of these relationships is derived from the animality of the passions as both cause and effect of madness. This is largely because the passions were seen as something that affected both the body and the mind. Once more, we can take as our starting point Foucault's excellent notes on the classical period's theorising of madness and passion; and once more we can look to the transpositional nature of cinema's representation of madness as it holds these, and other images, at the same time and in the same space.

Foucault points out that, for the classical age, the passions represented the continuous possibility of madness.[23] Once more the underlying implication of this was, however, threat and breakdown. Any sense of the celebratory nature of madness had been replaced by the threat of uncontrolled/uncontrollable passions. However, the key point is not simply that passion causes madness (and vice versa), rather that passion, no matter how controlled, must always harbour the potential for madness. It would seem that for this period of the Enlightenment, and for what came after, where passion is, madness follows.

We can find many examples of this attitude towards madness and passion in cinema. That is, not just the relationship between madness and passion, but also the potential for madness, existing on the edge of madness, through the intervention of passion. A great many of the cinematic images of this version of madness follow the culturally inscribed ideas that rational and logical thought is primary to the (Eurocentric) masculine, and passionate, emotion-driven feelings are primary to the feminine. Furthermore, the masculine is defined through the mind, the feminine through the body. Such binarisms operate in part because they have been so effectively encoded cinematically and in a great variety of other discourses. Since at least the Middle Ages in western thought, women have been aligned with madness and passion – an alignment that has taken many forms (from witchcraft in the Middle Ages to hysteria in the twentieth century). So it is not altogether surprising to see it continued in cinema's representations. Even in a genre where there is a socialised sensibility about the passions – such as film *noir* – women's actions verge on madness, and position the men who are tempted by them as equally mad. Cora, in *The Postman Always Rings Twice* (Garnett 1946; Rafelson 1981), inflames passion and mad acts.

All of this is relatively apparent – we are used to the images and ideas that passion unhinges the rational mind, and that the feminine is closer to this passionate world of emotions. (It is an image that follows the depiction of women in western culture as the one most easily tempted, and tempting, most corporeally driven and most corporeally seductive, and so on). A great deal of the cinematic representation of madness' relationship to passion follows this line. This includes the masculine passions causing madness as well as the feminine as passion embodied. It is even quite straightforward to map out how these representations are in keeping with the cultural line of thought that the negativity of such relations are due to their perceived lack of productivity. Note, for example, how it is the intervention of the feminine (as passion) that causes near madness in the male protagonist and a lack of production in film *noir*. It is interesting to note how this seems to be sometimes inverted, and madness and passion are seen as necessary values for productivity. The machine in *The Terminator* (Cameron 1984) and *Terminator 2* (Cameron 1991), along with Sarah Conner (John's mother), become more effective (that is, more productive) when they act with passion. Sarah is seen in terms of a whole range of mad/passionate registers: she is socially outcast as mad; medically committed to a psychiatric hospital (where she is represented as coldly rational to the point of insanity); and dispassionate about her son. It is only when her passion is allowed that she can become productive (that is, save the world) once more. Another version of this is Zorg's lack of productivity until the intervention of the passionate madness of Betty in *Betty Blue*. Such contradictory practices in these examples (the productive versus the counter productive of passion and madness) demonstrate that cinema produces versions of madness that see it as destructive and creative. For as many examples we might find in film of the disruptive negativities of passion and madness, there are an equal number of examples that show them as fundamental to our lives. However, there are certain aspects to these representations that make them less straightforward than first appears.

The disruptive forces of madness and passion can be figured as a necessary part of the narrative. Lives stall, solutions to crimes remain impenetrable, emotions are restrained and repressed, until passion is introduced. This level of productivity is one of the ways cinematic narrative distinguishes between passion and madness, and when it does we see legacies of classical and nineteenth-century lines of thought. Passion that is controlled and monitored can be productive, but once it exceeds that point it becomes madness and its productivity is brought into question. Here, we find a line directly from the classical age – passion drives us mad, a little passion can be productive. The aim then becomes how to keep the passions in check, render them productive, so as to prevent madness. Work, it was argued, would be the cure for madness: 'On the savage's side, immediate desire, without discipline, without constraint, without real morality; on the laborer's side, pleasure without mediation, in other words, without vain stimulus, without provocation or imaginary achievement' (Foucault 1987: 193). Note this in terms of the cinematic examples given above: Zorg does become productive through Betty's passionate madness, but only after her death and, consequently, the passion is held in check; Sarah's return to the passionate in order to save the world is a passion constrained in terms of motherhood. And this is not a view simply within the classical period. If we take the Gothic/Romantic tradition (as a type of antithetical position) madness and passion retain their sense of potential productivity for only as long as they are restrained. Dr Frankenstein is the perfect example of this – no one doubts his productivity, but once obsession takes over it is a warped and perverted production filled with madness. This is the legacy we still find dominating certain representations of madness in the cinematic imagination.

Fear

We have already made note of the forceful influence that fear has had in the West's attitude towards madness from the beginning of the eighteenth century onwards. And fear has featured prominently in cinema's representation of madness. However, it not simply the fear of madness, its unpredictability, the implied sense of violence, the disruptive force, that carries this aspect of the representation. It is also the fear that in madness exists not the distant, removed other, but the self. In these terms it is attached to passion. One of the things that make the representations of the excesses of passion so compelling is that it is a version of emotions that the spectator has expressed and experienced before. And in this self-recognition lies the fear of that excess and madness.

Cinematic representations of the fear of madness often carry with them this associative process – madness is to be feared and made separate, but at the same time it is perpetually linked to the central protagonists. They are not not mad because they fear madness, but rather they constantly display the potential for madness because of these fears. The hunted teenagers in the slasher films have a specified link to the killer, often including, significantly, the possibility of one of the group being the mad person, or being driven mad by the events.[24] This is the fear of suburbia gone mad, of what is known and understandable suddenly becoming irrational and threatening. In this we witness a version of what Foucault called the Great Fear, where madness became something that spreads from its confinement into the social order:

> Suddenly, in a few years in the middle of the eighteenth century, a fear arose – a fear formulated in medical terms but animated, basically by a moral myth. People were in dread of a mysterious disease that spread, it was said, from the houses of confinement and would soon threaten the cities. . . The evil that men had attempted to exclude by confinement reappeared, to the horror of the public, in a fantastic guise. There appeared, ramifying in every direction, the themes of an evil, both physical and moral, that enveloped in this very ambiguity the mingled powers of corrosion and horror.
>
> (Foucault 1987: 202; 203)

This is the same type of moral corrosion that we find in both the slasher and serial killer films. It is not just the mad who have their morality questioned, but their acts also bring into question the morality of the good person.

The fear then becomes not simply one of going mad, but of becoming immoral, of losing that which socialises and retains the sensibility of the human as prescribed in the philosophical – and medical – terms of the classical age. In this sense, even if at the textual level these sorts of films may seem postmodern in style, their philosophical, moral and ideological standpoint is one from the eighteenth century. They continue both the medicalisation of madness (that is, something to be contained within a socially organised discourse of the rational) and the phenomenon of placing the mad on display. Furthermore, this is the case not just within these film genres, but is also to be found in a much wider range. The capacity for madness to induce passionate excess, to bring into question the moral order, to undermine the modes of production, and so on, are elements that recur in cinema across the full generic and textual range.

There is a triple agenda to this relationship of fear to madness (originating from the classical age). The first two we have noted above – the fear of madness (and what it can do to the rational mind), and the fear of confinement if one became mad (Foucault's idea of the birth of the asylum). The third aspect of fear and madness comes from the medical theories that were developed for treatment: 'Fear, in the eighteenth century, was regarded as one of the passions most advisable to arouse in madmen. It was considered the natural complement of the constraints imposed upon maniacs and lunatics' (Foucault 1987: 180). In the cinematic examples we have employed so far this same insertion of fear can be seen – only this time it originates from a number of different sources, including the cinematic itself. It may be a little too much to suggest that cinema performs the same sort of social and individual fear-inducing effects that the asylum did in the eighteenth and nineteenth centuries; but it can be argued that the basis of the fear that is represented in such films as the slasher and serial killer originates from this period. In other words, the fear the spectator experiences is an intended one, one to be aroused as part of the experience of watching the representation of madness. Of course it is different from this other version, the one that forms part of the confinement. And yet at one level the purpose and intent is remarkably similar. Fear, along with the other passions, confines us, the spectator, within the cinematic apparatus. We desire these passions because they are what enable the act of spectating to actually take place – this is the psychic commitment to the film itself. This is part of the idea of identification of the spectator as madness that will be so essential for much of this book.

Resistances

If the debate so far signals some of the ways in which various discourses of madness have become part of the cinematic representation of the mad, we now need to acknowledge that there is also a resistance to such attempts in these representations.

Madness is that which resists representation. Part of what needs to be determined here is the position of the spectator in these resistances. If madness is figured as resistance, and cinema attempts to produce representations of madness, between the two is the spectator, whose function is to move between inadequate representations and seductive resistances. In this way, the act of the spectator is both to contribute to, and negate, these actions. The spectator performs a type of semiotic construction in the representation of madness, filling out the images, constructing the diegetics. At the same time, he/she engages in the resistances of madness, in part because they must share in the same resistant function. Just as it is part of being a spectator to construct (and reconstruct) representations, so it is also to resist. And it is in such resistances to the text that we can see comparable attributes of the mad. In the spectator's resistance to meaning, the image, the narrative forces, and so forth, we find acts of madness – not madness itself, but sensibilities that, in any other context, would be considered mad.

The sense, and presence, of resistance is one of the fundamental aspects of psychoanalysis; for Freud it was part of the very constitution and operation of the unconscious. Resistance is what enables the unconscious to exist, and what makes psychoanalysis necessary. By its very existence the unconscious resists meaning and interpretation, almost as if this was part of its primary function. Part of the aim of this section will be to consider how cinema also contains a similar sense of resistance to meaning that, in this case, becomes part of its pleasures. What such resistances are – what is being resisted, how the resistance itself is constituted, and so on – in such pleasures become complicated not just because they are made up of a variety of sources and activities, including the diversity of the textual and the act of spectating. Complexity also originates from the very idea of resistance. Here we have something, essential to the act of watching a film, which originates from different processes, including:

- Resistances to interpretation from the narrative field of a film. This would include how narrative sets up ways to enigmatise itself. When we watch a film (and it does not necessarily have to be something as obvious as a thriller or mystery) there are elements in the narrative that purposefully allow for a resistance to interpretation. Some of these will eventually be resolved, but others will remain open and even unresolvable. These elements of the narrative will challenge the very process of interpretation because their function is to resist.

- Resistances to reading the narrative itself. Apart from narrative elements setting up sites of resistance, there are also processes within the act of spectating that perform similar functions. Sometimes it is immensely pleasurable to resist, and this resistance can be developed by the spectator for a number of different reasons and purposes. There can be a resistance to the ways in which the narrative is going (we may not like particular eventualities and sequences, for example), or how resolutions are constructed. A meaning or interpretation given within the film may be unacceptable to the spectator and he/she will resist allowing this to have the supposed status of resolution. This can be from something as simple and obvious as narrative events (I do not want these characters to die in this way in Penn's version of *Bonnie and Clyde* or this ending of *Chinatown* (Polanski 1974)) to a more complex variation of cultural/ideological resistance to history (the rewriting of Vietnam in the military genre of the 1980s in Hollywood). Such resistances can also involve a political agenda for the spectator. Counter-reading patriarchal and phallocentric film is a resistance through ideological pleasures.

- The resistance to pleasure. Censorship or guilt can operate at both the cultural and individual level. Either way such reactions carry within them a sense of resistance that sometimes is based on pleasure. The representations of sex (or certain sexual activities), once censored, form guilty pleasures; the body becomes a site for the playing out of resistances to pleasure and the source of these same pleasures. The body of Bardot, for example, in the 1950s and 1960s is censored because it is too pleasurable (and it is a particular type of woman's pleasure); it thus also becomes, at the same time, something to resist. The pornographic image is continually set up as a resistance to a type of pleasure that is excessive. The greater the sense of excess the stronger the resistance.

- Resistances to closure and finitude. A different type of resistance, yet one related to pleasure, is the one towards closure of narrative and the finitude of spectatorship. One of the fundamental aspects of resistance and pleasure in cinema is that it allows for a playing out of precisely these attributes. In other words, part of the reason we watch films is to play out the acts of resistance, experience the pleasures of both having resistances and giving into them. This particular pleasure does not give in to closure and so we repeat the experience. This is made even more imperative because all narratives contain within them a sense of closure – the ending is always about (from the story of the individual to apocalypse itself).

There are many more types of resistance in cinema, but these examples will do for now. What we need to map out is the process of resistance itself and how the psychoanalytic model can be seen in the spectator's watching of a film. In this we move from the resistances to representing madness, as noted in the first part of this chapter, to madness' inherent motivation of resistance to representation and interpretation. From this we can take up other interpretative positions, including the spectator as neurotic, psychotic and hysteric.

Freud's *The Interpretation of Dreams* (1985) is full of instances where resistance is of primary concern. In fact, this text represents one of the most sustained discussions of the operation of resistance in and to psychoanalysis in any of Freud's works. After all, Freud acknowledges that what he is dealing with in dreams is a type of psychic activity that is resistant to interpretation by design. The attributes and qualities of resistances Freud notes include distortion, doubt, interruption, forgetting, hostility, addition through after-thought, alienation, condensation, displacement, and disguise.[25] These, Freud argues, are all part of the resistance that the subject brings to the scene of analysis in order to resist, perhaps even deny, interpretation. Beyond this is another type of resistance – something which is an integral part of the dream itself – that Freud calls the navel

> There is at least one spot in every dream at which it is unplumbable – a navel, as it were, that is its point of contact with the unknown' and 'There is often a passage in even the most thoroughly interpreted dream which has to be left obscure; this is because we become aware during the work of interpretation that at that point there is a tangle of dream-thoughts which cannot be unraveled and which moreover adds nothing to the contents of the dream. This is the dream's navel, the spot where it reaches down into the unknown.
>
> (Freud 1985: 186; 671)

The point of this navel, then, is resistance itself because it is not just the unknown (for Freud, for indeed anyone), it is also the unknowable. Our concern here is cinema's navel, of those moments where a film reaches into an unknown/unknowable point, and how we recognise them and distinguish them from say a point that is interpretatively complex or different. For part of the function of a film is to establish a resistance to interpretation – even in the most obvious of ways. Where is the pleasure, after all, if we know all that there is to know about a film before, during, and after we watch it?

What all of this brings into play is not just understanding a film, getting its point (if there is such a thing) or even a sense of what it means, but how we interpret things. To speak of resistances in cinema (cinema's resistance to interpretation, the various resistances of being a spectator, the sites of cultural resistances, and so on) is also to speak of the analytic processes. Madness is our exemplar here because it presents the most extreme form of resistance to analysis. This does not mean an impossibility of analysis, or a negation of it, but a challenge to what constitutes analysis itself. Similarly, cinema can be seen as a type of resistance to what constitutes analysis and, like madness, ends up producing new types of analytic processes.

Part of the resistance that we are speaking of here is to do with resolution, with solving the enigmatic, and acknowledging those parts that are the navel of the film. This is the exchange of solutions – those offered by the cinematic apparatus (including cinema as a medium, the cultural and historical aspects, intertextual processes, and so forth), by the film itself (the constant unfolding of the narrative, the micro-resolutions and revelations about events and sequences), and those brought to the film by the spectator. Here is the equivalent beauty of this in Freud, via Derrida:

> we must recall that everything here is *concentrated* and at the same time *dissolved* in a solution (*Lösung*), a chemical solution but also – and Freud takes this sense into account in the interpretation of his dream – the solution of a problem (it's the same word, *Lösung*), an analytic solution. An analytic solution untangles, resolves, even absolves; it undoes the symptomatic or etiological knot.
>
> (Derrida 1998: 7)

All of this sense of a solution stands alongside the navel that cannot be solved because often it is not the solution that is being prepared, but the act of analysis. This, once more, is the pleasure.

This line out of Freud through Derrida is worth pursuing, for it is contiguous with many of the points raised so far and that will continue to be of interest here. If there is this navel to dreams, and films, which is acknowledged as the point of the unknown, and beyond that, as unknowable, then part of its function is to hold up interpretation and test the analytic processes. Thus, it brings into question what it is to analyse, to posit interpretation, to make sense of the text and its elements. This is what Freud sees as the internal resistances, and what Derrida sees as the point of the whole thing:

> However, like the resistance that we meet with in analysis, this relation of forces *has meaning. And truth.* . . . . Resistance must be interpreted; it has as much meaning as what it opposes; it is just as charged with meaning and thus just as interpretable as that which it disguises or displaces.
>
> (Derrida 1998: 13)

Of course, the cleverest of resistance is that which draws no attention to itself. There will be that which resists in the most forceful of ways, such as the seeming narrative of *Un chien andalou*, time and memory in *Last Year at Marienbad* (Resnais 1961), reality and dream in *Blood of a Poet*, the soliloquies on the pointlessness of events in *The Thin Red Line* (Malick 1998), or even something as unresolved as the ending of *Lost Highway* (1997) and the loss of the sense of identity in *Mulholland Drive* (Lynch 2001). There is that which feigns resistance to engineer the spectator's desire for solution, such as the utterance and pursuit of Rosebud in *Citizen Kane* (Welles 1941), Lester Burnham's opening statement that he will be dead in a year in *American Beauty* (Mendes 1999). And then there will be those resistances that remain undeclared unless the spectator takes them up and attempts to read them through. These are the moments and images in the film that the spectator directly contrives and constructs from his/her own position as the distiller of solutions.

No matter what level of resistance we are speaking of here, Derrida's point holds true – the resistance has meaning in itself, just as what it resists has meaning (remembering that what is at hand is the resistance to meaning and interpretation). Within this we find the comparable attributes of madness, cinema, and madness alongside cinema. That is, madness is resistance to meaning in the Symbolic; cinema is resistance to ontological certainty (that is, as spectator we slip from various points of reality into various points of constructed narrative and psychic realities) as well as meaning (no matter how many meanings we generate out of a film there will never be one that can stand as the finalised, resolved, unequivocal meaning); and madness and cinema share resistances to the idea that representational systems and constructions of meaning are, or ever can be, unifying and universalising systems. These are the dynamics between system and articulation that revolve around resistance and meaning. Cinema and madness are paradigms of resistance to analysis, and each film and each act of madness is the articulation of such resistances. In themselves – the film and the mad act – are also resistances to the larger paradigm. Each film offers up a point of resistance to cinema, as well as with the analysis of the film and its elements. This type of resistance is also a type of aporia and excess. Aporia is that which marks a point that cannot be resolved. It is a certain difficulty or dilemma that presents no solutions, only further puzzlement. Within this lies much of the pleasure of becoming the spectator of a film.

Our line of thought here has developed out of the difficulties of representing madness, the confluence of madness and cinema, and of the resistances to both representation and analysis that both these present. We commenced this chapter with a sense of the difficulties and impossibilities of representing madness and how, by considering some of the representational processes, we gain insight into cinema itself. This is not simply an issue of choosing a subject matter that resists representation, but rather of looking towards a sort of madness in cinema, a madness of cinema. This will lead us to consider how cinema is constituted not just of its films, but also of the construction and actions of the spectator. In the following chapters, our concern will be focused on how the spectator as a type of subjectivity operates within cinema, forming a model that compares to madness.

CHAPTER 3

The Neurotic Spectator who Eroticises

I had a kind of dread of him, for he was obviously fond of cruelty
(Freud 1990b: 47)

This chapter, and the following two, represent three 'versions' of the film spectator located in a site of madness. Our concern here is the ways in which the cinematic spectator is formed within a context of obsession and neurosis. This will be followed by a chapter on spectatorship and transgression (psychosis), and one on spectatorship and the body (hysteria). All three chapters have the common aim of considering how the cinema spectator can be reinterpreted as involving the sorts of madness discussed in the opening chapter. Further, we are also interested in why and how there can be pleasure in experiencing images and narratives that cause displeasure. To arrive at this we must initially work through some of the issues of obsessional neurosis, tracking some of the key points.

Obsessional neurotics walk amongst us; and it is this aspect, for Freud, that presents one of the greatest interpretative difficulties. At the beginning of the 'Rat Man' case study (Freud 1990b), Freud argues that obsessional neurosis, as a language, is easier to 'read' than hysteria (he actually calls it a dialect of hysteria), but is far less often encountered. This is because obsessional neurotics 'dissimulate their condition in daily life' (Freud 1990b: 38). So here we have a form of madness that can exist with little trouble in the everyday world. This is not simply because it is so easily disguised, or that it can be passed off quite readily as the actions of normalcy – although both of these are certainly part of the process. It is also because in the obsessional neurotic lies some reflection, some manifestation, of the actions of everyone. Each of us is capable of being obsessive, so what is this moment that transforms the manageable, even enjoyable, obsession into a neurosis? The most obvious answer would be that moment when it comes to dominate all our actions and thoughts, leading us to act in ways that are counter to everyday living; and for psychoanalysis this is the case. But what of the obsessions that we are unaware of? What of those that cajole our thoughts in unseen ways? And what of the systems and ideas that operate outside of the psychoanalytic field?

For the obsessed, their desire exists, to a certain degree, beyond any moral imperative. It is an obsession first and foremost. It is only afterwards that any sense of morality regarding the issues may follow. And yet part of the neurotic attribute of obsession is entwined in a moral universe, for the obsessions are usually linked to some sense of moral concern and/or fear, often stemming from a conflict with authority (such as the Father). It is precisely this moment of conflict (often at the level of morality) that makes the obsessional neurosis appear as madness. This is in turn tied up with the continual repetition of seemingly meaningless acts. Yet, there is also meaning here, and of an order that can often follow very specific rules and codes of practice. So many of the representations of obsessive behaviour (in both psychoanalytic case studies and cinema) have a moral framework that is employed to either represent the obsessions or explain them. In the extensive inventory of obsessions that the Rat Man displays, Freud continually tracks them back to conflicts of a sexual and/or authoritative origin. The obsessions, the Rat Man himself points out, are derived from a need to protect two figures he loves – his father and a woman friend. The compulsions to act in certain ways and perform certain deeds are talismans that originate from a conflict between the moral and the immoral. All of the Rat Man's obsessive acts (protecting his 'lady', getting slim, understanding all words spoken to him, and counting between thunderclaps) are developed through a fear of punishment or a sense of making things right.

John Doe, the serial killer, in *Se7en*, and Travis Bickle, in *Taxi Driver*, show similar attributes in their compulsive behaviour to what Freud describes in regard to the Rat Man. Both are driven by the same strong sense of the moral. However, for them the focus switches from a universal version – the desire to clean the immorality from the streets – to specific manifestations and back again. This is a desire turned into a form of obsession that is highly codified. For John Doe, it is mapped out through the meticulously planned performance of the seven deadly sins; for Travis Bickle it is the acting out of the obsession to protect a woman.[26] Like the Rat Man, both Bickle and John Doe retain the sense of conflict between how they act (the morally driven) and how the social order reads such acts. It is important to both of them that their actions are played out within a socio-political sphere. The one variation of this is that John Doe and Bickle seem beyond the internal conflict of the moral and evil self that Freud speaks of (Freud 1990b: 58), and instead this is projected onto, and so played out through, the character of David Mills in *Se7en* and Betsy in *Taxi Driver*.

These three obsessional neurotics – the Rat Man, John Doe, and Travis Bickle, also demonstrate another common feature of excessive compulsions. Freud argues that true obsessional acts are auto-erotic, and that part of the repressed sexual development of this is tied to the scopophilic (the obsessed pleasure of looking) and epistemophilic (the obsessed pleasure for knowledge) drives (see, for example, Freud 1990b: 124). The epistemophilic drive (that of knowing, of the need to know and to have knowledge) is present in all three, but is performed in different ways. (This performative function is part of the epistemophilia and is linked to the origins of the obsessions). John Doe knows everything about his obsessions and the meanings attached to them, and the film's narrative plays out that knowledge against the lack of knowledge of the police and his victims.[27] Travis Bickle is convinced that only he has the true knowledge of the sordidness of the world. It is noteworthy that his diary entries and voice-overs contain no comments on the fact that no one else sees the world in this way. This is because they acts as knowledge for him rather than a personal interpretation. His vision of ridding the city of its sins is the one thing that retains certainty in his world order. The Rat Man knows the least (at a conscious level) about why he acts the way he does, but like the others what he does know is that the obsessive acts *must* be carried out. For these obsessional neurotics, the relationship to epistemophilia is derived from conflict – the certainty about what one does (and why it has to be done) against the disjunction of these acts in the social order. The fact that John Doe seems least in conflict with this (for example, his calmness in the back of the police car as they drive out across the plains[28], and his placidity when he gives himself up) is further evidence that it is David Mills who becomes the compulsively driven subject when he understands not only that his wife is dead, but also how she died.

There is a further resonance here. What these figures of neurosis and obsession present is a conflict based on a compulsion that is seemingly insatiable and originates from a conflict of pleasure and guilt, the inescapable compulsion and the forbidding authority. It is worth following this line for a moment longer and comparing another of Freud's obsessional patients. After this, we can then turn to the act of the cinematic spectator as a type of neurosis. A footnote, in Freud, describes how this man accidentally kicked his foot on a branch whilst walking in a park. He became worried that someone else would injure themselves on it:

> He picked it up and flung it into the hedge that bordered the path. On his way home he was suddenly seized with uneasiness that the branch in its new position might perhaps be projecting a little from the hedge and might cause injury to some one passing by the same place after him. He was obliged to jump off his tram, hurry back to the park, find the place again, and put the branch back in its former position.
>
> (Freud 1990b: 73)

Freud then points out that this action in fact makes the branch more dangerous than where he had thrown it, but the obsessive could not see this; Freud describes this as a hostile act. The acts of Bickle and John Doe are of the same order and are derived from an obsession that is of a completely different moral order to the ones inhabited by the other characters. Their actions are driven by an obsession to rid the world of crime and sin, but their acts are hostile and at least as dangerous as the ones they seek to do away with. And it is here that we see that curious mix of disgust and pleasure within the compulsions themselves. To follow this further we must now turn to a different perspective on this same theme, and in doing so move more towards the issue of neurosis itself.

The erotics between pleasure and anxiety

It is important that a sense of the relationship between neurosis, obsession, and anxiety is outlined here. This next section will cover some of the fundamental aspects of Freud's ideas on this subject. It is a topic that has a rather long history in Freud's writings so part of the agenda will be to untangle how psychoanalysis positions anxiety (*Angst*) in terms of the ego and the libido – that is, with the (obsessive) agencies of the self and pleasure. In

Freud's reading of *Gradiva* we find part of the ongoing process of rethinking the relationship between the libido and *Angst*.[29] Freud's initial theorising of this relationship was that *Angst* was a direct transformation of libido – a line he later abandoned. But the interpretation of the relationship between the two in *Gradiva* is less categorical and more fluid. For here, we read that *Angst* and libido are connected, and not a transformation of one for the other. As Freud puts it: 'The *Angst* in *Angst*-dreams, like neurotic *Angst* in general, corresponds to a sexual affect, a libidinal feeling, and arises out of the libido by a process of repression' (Freud 1990a: 85, translation modified). Even so, Freud is, by this time (1926), offering a different sort of interpretation – yet he never totally abandons the idea that connections between libidinal drives and *Angst* exist in some form. Let's follow Freud a little further in this issue, for his brilliance at creating problems within his own theorising leads to an interesting set of connections.

Freud questions his own ideas on the transformation of libidinal drives into *Angst* mainly because he comes around to argue that the source of *Angst* is from the ego (with its dominance of the sense of self) rather than the id (where the libido resides). This, in turn, allows him to posit that it is an issue of different types of *Angst* – that of the ego and that of the id (see, for example, Freud 1987: 320–1) – and that the ego-*Angst* must utilise psychical energy that is desexualised. Freud's reasoning here is difficult to summarise, but at the core of the argument is the idea of defence. By arguing that *Angst* is ego based, Freud sees a relationship between the preservation of the self through the recognition of danger. Still, Freud does not dismiss the idea of id-*Angst*, and its shadowy possibilities remain. Freud's issue is with origins – the issue of aetiology that appears at the outset (in 1895) and eventually leads to this theorising of an ego-based *Angst*. Finally, Freud offers a solution that allows for both ego and libidinal processes. *Angst* is ego derived, and therefore tied to flight from danger as an act of self-preservation, and at the same time it has an origin in the repression of libidinal urges. Freud's answer is that in neurotic *Angst* we find that the ego 'is making a similar attempt at flight from the demand by its libido, that it is treating this internal danger as though it were an external one' (Freud 1986: 453). This further reveals the internal conflict involved in the neurotic *Angst*.

All of these distinctions take place in Freud's work (most notably in the Addenda to *Inhibitions, Symptoms and Angst*, Freud 1987) within the context of realistic *Angst* and a neurotic *Angst*. Here Freud draws our attention to the difference between *Angst*, which has a lack of an object, yet still has intentionality, and *Furcht* (fear), where an object has been established (see Freud 1998: 324–5). Neither are privileged as lying more in the domain of the realistic *Angst*, although relationships shift according to such positionings. It is in this set of ideas that we can return to the issue of the film text. For Freud, *Angst* is either derived from a real situation, or it is derived from a neurosis (hence a type of psychical reality determined within the neurosis). Objects of fear direct such feelings with an indistinguishable intensity, so that they can appear just as real to those experiencing either form; just as the objects of fear can be frightening whether they actually exist or not. Lacan's take on this follows Freud, especially when he is dealing with the relationship of the object to the causal processes of *Angst*. His is a semiotic reading that continues the line of Freud's ego-based interpretation. Hence: '*Angst* is always defined as appearing suddenly, as arising. To each of the objectal relations there corresponds a mode of identification of which *Angst* is the signal. The identifications in question here precede the ego-identification' (Lacan 1988a: 68–9 translation modified). This idea of a level of identification preceding the ego allows Lacan to emphasise the primitive aspects of *Angst* – in effect the id-based aspects of the fears, terrors, and even seductions. For let's not forget that there is potentially always something deeply seductive about sensations of *Angst*; and it would seem quite likely that much of this is derived from the libidinal as much as the ego. True seduction, it could be argued, exists in this intersection of the libidinally charged and the sense of the self.

Two more features of *Angst* need to be noted before we can move on. *Angst* is a central component to neurosis – not just in the *Angst* neurosis that Freud defines as a particular type of neurosis, but of neurotic acts overall. It is not the existence of *Angst*, however, that indicates neurosis, but rather the force and persistence of the feelings. This means that the difference between 'normal' feelings of *Angst* and neurosis can be either the force of the feelings or the overwhelming persistence of them, or a combination of the two. In this sense, realistic *Angst* may not have anything to do with the reality of the fears and dangers (that is whether or not there is actually something to be anxious about), but if they are understandable within the contexts in which they take place. This raises the second point. Freud, at various times, discusses issues such as the social background to types of *Angst*, and the appearance of *Angst* in children. These sorts of 'histories' allow for a sense of understandable (that is realistic) *Angst*. When such states extend beyond the socially recognised, or persist with such intensity that they overtake the subject's existence, psychoanalysis defines them as neurotic.

When we introduce the filmic text into all this we seem to have a number of choices in terms of locating it and the spectator. Textual *Angst* could be posited alongside Freudian realistic *Angst*, because it exists in part as a social process, in part as a semiotically coded form, and in part because it is a noted form of reading. In this sense, the text has taken up the status of objectal relations; and this, in turn, raises the issue of what constitutes the object of *Angst*. Is it the whole film, various combinations of elements within it, or some very specific objects within the film itself? Given the centrality of the ego in this reading we must also account for the acts of spectatorship. These are issues we will need to return to later.

An alternative to this is that we might want to argue that textual *Angst* is far more like a neurotic variation because it does not actually exist in the external world, and its quasi-real status is often acknowledged before, during, and after the act of spectating. We might want to argue that textual *Angst* inhabits a realm that combines both types, operating with elements of the realistic and neurotic. All of this can also be applied to the attachment of fear to certain types of objects. It is these issues that will concern us for the next few moments.

It is significant that *Gradiva* is Freud's reading of a text; and in this analysis he argues that not only is it possible, but indeed highly effective, to use texts in the same way as a psychoanalyst might analyse a person's psychical processes. This issue of the textual has many possible inflections, and the one we want to take up here is the relationship between libidinally derived (and charged) id-*Angst* and the textual aetiology of these feelings. At one level, this might offer some interpretation of why there is pleasure in watching images of displeasure or becoming terrified by watching a film; but perhaps of greater significance is the possibility that this may provide a reading of the elicitation of pleasure through fear. This, then, is the moment where conflict becomes attraction, and leads us not entirely to a return to Freud's ideas of transformation and *Angst* – but not a rejection either.

Angst, pleasure and the cinema

The first model to be taken up here is the idea of textual *Angst* as a function of id-*Angst*. It is possible to negotiate Freud's original problem of the ego-based source of *Angst* because what defines this textual/id-*Angst* is precisely what Freud saw for much of his theorising of this concept. In other words, the *Angst* a spectator *creates* from a film (or experiences from watching the film – although there are some profound differences here) can be seen as a type of transformation of the libidinal processes. *Creates* because we must not lose sight of the acts of being a spectator and the force of such acts in the formation of any pleasures and displeasures in a film. It should be noted that this is not a simple attempt to recoup the original conceptualisations in Freud, but rather a way of developing the differences in this process. What allows us to do this is that the film declares its libidinal status – it wants us to desire it, it needs desire in order to function, and so on. The idea that the *Angst* in/of a film is tied to a libidinal drive is often never far from its surface. And the greater the fear and anxiety created and invested in that moment of the film, the greater the need for seduction and desire. Perhaps unconsciously Freud allows for such a path to be opened up.

To return to the *Gradiva* lines cited earlier, *Angst*-dreams are compared to the *Angst* of neurosis – and these dreams most strongly resemble the film. The cause of the *Angst* is not simply the dream (or, for us, the film) in *Gradiva*, but the relationship between film and spectator. Recalling that this is a period when Freud is still holding to the idea of the libido as transformed into *Angst*, this is why he states: 'When we interpret a dream, therefore, we must replace *Angst* by sexual excitement' (Freud 1990a: 85, translation modified). Our model thus becomes one where *Angst* is an essential component in becoming a spectator of a film – and not just films that create *Angst*, but all films, all spectating experiences have this attribute. This suggests that there is no need for anxiety, no requirement of displeasure and discomfort, for the operation of this seductive element. In being a spectator there is always a presence of *Angst* at some level. It is part of what allows for the emotive attachment to the film, as well as part of the narrative

construction. In other words, narrative exists because of a level of
Angst in the spectator, because this is where the commitment to the
text takes place. In order to understand this more fully the next
part will consider two versions of *Angst* – realistic and neurotic – in
terms of the spectator.

Realistic *Angst* and the film/spectator

Freud defines realistic *Angst* not simply as that which exists in the
real world, but as something 'very rational and intelligible' (Freud
1986: 441). A real presence of danger will understandably produce
this form of *Angst*, but so too will any perceived sense of threat
even if it has no basis in reality. In this way we need to speak of the
reality of *Angst* independent of its origins of textuality or the
outside world, for it is always ultimately an issue of psychic reality.
And from this follows the idea that *Angst* generated from a film
shares many of the same qualities of those feelings generated by
real threats. The moment of terror, to select the most transparent
of examples, on the screen has these attributes of rationality and
intelligibility, in part from the textual constructions (such as
generic conventions, narrative devices), and in part from the acts
that the spectator performs. *Angst* does not simply emerge from
the screen, nor is it entirely textually devised. For those moments
of *Angst* to take place, the spectator must be a willing participant
and co-creator. It is in this productive process that we find the reality of the terrors and fears. In this sense, the scenes of horror do
not create horror, the moments of terror hold no terrors, the
excitements of passion are only the ordinary, until the spectator,
which requires an initial investment and transformation of
erotism, transforms them into realistic *Angst*.

This idea of erotism is used in an etymological sense of love; so
we love our *Angst*. It is also used here in Lacan's sense of *erotisation*,
when the subject places great emphasis on a particular signifier.
Furthermore, as with the psychotic words of Schreber, such as
Seelenmord (soul murder), this erotisation is self-reflexive: 'When the
signifier finds itself charged thus, the subject is perfectly well aware
of it' (Lacan 1993: 55). In the spectator's erotics of *Angst* – which can
be seen as a type of neurosis – we find an attachment to the charged
signifier that is derived from a psychical origin of the spectator. It
should be noted that this does not exclude the cultural processes
involved, for these are an integral part of the spectating position.

This emphasises even more so the question of why would we want to participate in such activity? This is not just why would we want to position ourselves to experience such pain and fear, but why would we become active agents in its creation? Two of the reasons that have been touched on so far may be summarised as: firstly, that the flow between libidinal drives and *Angst* means that the two are often merged. In this sense *Angst* is associated with pleasure and (often sexual) release. Secondly, the terror on the screen (to continue the example) only becomes terrifying through the actions of the spectator, thus giving the whole sequence a sense of creation. This is the id-based *Angst*, as distinct from the libidinal, which locates the spectator's ego (that is, sense of self) within the textual dynamics. From this the spectator gains a sense of control over the terror. In other words, the *Angst* is made realistic, and has an investment in being such, by the act of spectating. This is the pleasure of creating a type of real (which includes a sense of reality as well as versions of realism) out of textually-driven *Angst*. Here we witness a version of *Fort/da*, where pleasure can only be derived out of a sense of control and revenge. In Freud's reading of the child with the spool, the acts of revenge by the child on the mother requires him to acknowledge the *Angst* of loss and separation in order to gain a sense of control and pleasure; just as the spectator must become terrified by the images on the screen in order to eroticise them.

Further to this is the id-*Angst* of the spectator as it becomes aligned to the various models of terror on the screen. This is more than the simple replication of the spectator's id-based desires, but a conflation of the screen terror with the release of forbidden desires of the spectator. This links in with Freud's (earlier) view of *Angst* and its relationship to hysteria. Freud, in reviewing this position, states: 'For we consider what is responsible for the *Angst* in hysteria and other neuroses is the process of repression' (Freud 1964: 83). The function of the scene in the film becomes part of the escape from repression for the spectator as we participate in the very *Angst* that is part of the repressed. More significant than this, however, is the idea that this moment of conflation – the spasm of time when id-*Angst* is formed by the spectator and the film – yields the formation of the symptom.

Neurotic *Angst* and the film/spectator

Such a description of realistic *Angst* would seem to leave little scope for its neurotic variant, especially within this context of the spectator and the film. However, we are never far from neurosis when we experience the eroticisms (of feelings such as fears, sexuality, love, despair) of the screen, in part because of the textual dimensions and their relationship to reality. What is at hand here is not so much the *realism* (that is, manifestations and variants of reality) of the source of the *Angst*, but the ways in which it functions in the formation of a type of subjectivity. In this context, such a subject position is the film spectator deriving pleasure from sources of anxiety. This, in turn, raises the question of does such a position align itself with neurosis through such acts of spectatorship (in other words, are we performing some sort of neurotic act in our pleasures of visual *Angst*); or does the *Angst* induce some form of neurosis? Of course, the two are not necessarily oppositional, but what they both bring to the fore is the issue of the neurotic spectator and the development of such a spectating type.

Putting to one side this idea of histories of developments, our concern here is with the idea of the neurotic spectator's capacity to eroticise, that is to love and be attached to, *Angst*. This raises the question of how such a spectating position can eroticise anything; as Lacan points out: 'how can a transference be so easily generated in neurotics, when they are so fettered when it comes to love?' (Lacan 1988a: 142) (and so recalling psychoanalysis' idea that transference is always about love). At one level, the answer to such a question is what is being engaged with here. The idea of the neurotic spectator allows for the eroticisation of *Angst* because it is a position of love outside the culturally given. This completes the circle – the spectator creates the *Angst* in the film, imbues it with a form of love, this love foregrounds the neurotic qualities, which creates further *Angst* and greater attachment. All of this takes place within a curious inflection of love.

This love, that we specify as the spectator's neurotic love for his/her fear from, and within, the film, is following, and extending, Lacan's idea regarding the moment of love: 'That's what love is. It's one's own ego that one loves in love, one's own ego made real on the plane of the Imaginary' (Lacan 1988a: 142 translation modified). This is part of Lacan's idea that love is fundamentally part of the Imaginary processes – that is, formulated within the ego as a self-reflexive moment. Therefore, the spectator must eroticise his/her *Angst* not simply in order to cope with it, make it pleasurable or even be seduced by it. The spectator eroticises it because it provides a capacity for his/her subjectivity to be asserted. This is the ego of the spectator made real, which becomes part of the id-*Angst*. This helps to explain why we do not flee the sources and objects of fear and unpleasure, for they are a fundamental part of this neurotic act of love, and subsequently an assertion of the ego made real. It is also a fundamental aspect to the turning of such unpleasures into pleasure, of why we go to experience cinema. Such an idea allows us to put the cycle in reverse; our love of the *Angst* renders us neurotic spectators, and we are neurotic spectators because we love our *Angst*.

How perverse is this? Can we accept such a scenario if it locates us, the spectator, as an agent of the perverse? To some extent we are saved such a decision because the neurosis has no perversions. When Lacan asks us to wonder how neurotics make love, his answer lies in the distinction between neurosis and perversion: '*La névrose, c'est le rêve plutôt que la perversion*' (Lacan 1975: 80) (Neurosis is dreaming rather than perversion). Lacan goes on to argue that the neurotic dreams of having perversions, rather than actually having them. The spectator is thus saved the role of the one who has perversions, and can settle for the dreaming qualities of neurosis! The other side of this issue, the representation of perversions on the screen, emphasises the distinction between spectator and film, and in doing so allows one to desire the other. And this is the other of psychoanalysis – the *objet petit a* (the objects of otherness in desire) – that contains our desires and all possible (temporary and/or feigned) satisfactions of them. It is this aspect that provides another link in the chain from spectator to *Angst*, for in these signs of *Angst* reside the *objet petit a* of desire.

But why neurotic spectators? Why not see these processes following the line described by Klein in her analysis of libidinal fixations (which would seem a closer point of comparison)? Her conclusion is that these fixations 'determine the genesis of neurosis and also of sublimation and that for some time the two follow the same path. It is the force of repression which determines whether this path will lead to sublimation or turn aside to neurosis' (Klein 1988: 105). Such a reading would be far more in keeping with the usual sense of things – that cinema, like other textual forms, can be seen as a type of sublimation for repressed thoughts. This would also be in line with Freud's ideas regarding the function of Art (which can be extended to include a wide range of textual systems) as a process of sublimation.

The reason why such an approach is not followed here is that the idea of a neurotic spectator allows us to explore different facets of this experience, as well as positing a different type of spectating position, derived from a different type of subject position. Klein's idea that the path of libidinal fixation splits at one point, and most of us follow the direction of sublimation, is certainly not excluded within such a reading (nor, for that matter, is the idea of textual systems and sublimation). The neurosis of spectating is different from the acts of sublimation, even if at times the two are negotiating the same orders of repression and pleasures. This point of the subject position is of further significance, because cinema acts as a type of cultural sublimation, which can also be traced to the sublimations of the spectator. The neurosis of the spectator, on the other hand, has its origins in the erotics of the relationship between image and eye, which is that creative moment of viewing, interpretation, and forming knowledges. Thus neurosis actually becomes a unifying process between spectator and image.

It is important to remember that neurosis is both a compromise and part of a system of defence.[30] It is both compromise and defence because this is what is required to negotiate repression, and also to allow the neurotic subject to continue functioning. Without some compromise the neurotic passes into profound madness; without the acts of neuroses the neurotic is defenceless. Compromise and defence feature in the cinematic *Angst* and its formations of pleasure and love. They are components that allow the *Angst* to take place (cultural compromise dictates the signifiers of terror, or indeed pleasure, allowed, whilst the defence process functions in a hegemonic manner) as well as shaping its features and structures. In doing so both compromise and defensive processes become attached to the erotics of the *Angst*. What the spectator attempts to defend against can be something as literal as the terror on the screen, as necessary as the loving of the image, as well as the obsessional component to enjoying a film. All of these, in the erotics, become essential to the pleasure of the gaze. This is why the model of the neurotic spectator is not simply aligned to something as literal as being frightened in a horror film. Any pleasure derived from watching a film contains within it, at this level of neurosis, *Angst*. This is the neurosis of being a cinematic spectator that confirms our psychic instabilities. As one of Lacan's analysands once said: 'We are all mentally ill, but we are not all obliged to be mad' (see Roudinesco 1997: 368); and as Lacan

himself said: 'we all have a little something in common with delusionals' (Lacan 1993: 48). The formations and functions of both
compromise and defence in neurosis are devised around the relationships of the neurotic to reality. It is in these processes that we
find further scope for the analysis of the spectator.

The rupturing effect of cinema

The ideas dealt with so far here – that the spectator demonstrates
a type of neurosis through his/her love of the *Angst* created by
watching a film – has a further point of comparison with Freud's
work.[31] Two aspects of particular interest here are Freud's ideas
that the onset of neurosis is linked to a certain disposition, and
that the cause of such attacks are often linked to frustration, particularly in terms of love. We have, according to Freud, two paths
when presented with continuing frustration. We can employ the
pent up psychical tension into some act in the external world that
will give libidinal satisfaction, or we can transform that frustration
into a sublimated act. If either (or both) these acts fail there is the
danger of an introverted libido, which 'turns away from reality,
which, owing to the obstinate frustration, has lost its value for the
subject, and turns towards the life of phantasy' (Freud 1987: 120).
Such a scenario sets up a conflict between the internal world of the
psyche and the external world of reality; and from this conflict we
have neurosis.

Freud urged distinction between what he saw as the two types of
onsets of neurosis (the changes promoting the onset being either
an external experience or a gradual internal development).
However, he also insisted that the two types share a great deal, and
can be seen as essentially the same process in terms of the neurotic
attack. The intensity of the neurosis depends on the amount of
libidinal frustration, and the relative success of the displacement.[32]

Let us return to the neurotic spectator who loves his/her libid-
inally-charged *Angst* derived from the very act of spectating. At
one level, it is possible to read the types of displacements Freud
discusses as operating within this act of watching a film. This
would mean, in effect, that the neurotic moments of spectating
operate to keep in check a full onset of a neurotic attack. It
should be noted that this is not simply arguing that by watching
a film we experience a type of quasi-neurosis (a version of sublimation for example) which, in its weakened form plays out the

transformation of a propensity for a full neurosis. This may well take place at one level of becoming a spectator (it would, for example, be the cathartic effect), however, we are more interested in how the libidinal charging of *Angst* operates as a type of neurosis. This is the act of watching the film not as a safe playing out of neurosis through phantasies, but rather as a type of onset of neurosis. The freeing of some of the frustrations of reality that can take place in the watching of a film are commonly known (note the cultural version of this in the opulent musicals of Hollywood during the 1930s' Depression or the pleasurable investment in representations of sexuality). However, unless this functions within the very specific frustration tied to the neurosis, we are witnessing no more (and, it must be said, no less) than a type of ludic joy. The common aspect of these phenomena is the psychoanalytic view that everyone has to 'contend with the same tasks of mastering their libido' (Freud 1987: 126). At one level, film participates in this mastering effect, but at another it functions quite beyond such acts of containment. In fact, cinema can be seen as part of a rupturing process that resists such containment – not all films, but some that assert a type of excessive, revolutionary force. It is precisely because the onset of neurosis is linked to a specific frustration that we cannot easily speak of a universal experience of neurosis in the eroticisation of *Angst*.

So far, we have seen two of the types of onset of neurosis that Freud details (that of frustration and of fixation). The third type is what he describes as 'an inhibition in development' (Freud 1987: 124) and is of less interest to us here than the fourth type, which is an increase in the quantity of libido that causes an imbalance. This would seem to suggest that such an imbalance could be 'triggered' by watching a film, thus presenting the antithesis of the phantasy model and cathexsis (that is, the psychical investment in an act, object or idea). This is the old argument of, for example, sexually ravenous (or violent) people emerge after watching sexually explicit (or violent) images. However, such a reading is far too simplistic and presents untenable, perhaps even unworkable, conclusions. Rather, what is significant about this lies in those fundamental issues of neurosis that we have been tracking so far, that of conflict and compromise. The conflict is between the ego and libidinal drives; the compromise is the articulation of the neurotic elements (such as obsession). The conflict remains an internal one, but the reality of the created world order of the filmic text adds a further dimension. We would need to consider the difference, as well as the common points, between the frustrations of reality to the onset of neurosis and the frustrations of the created world order of the film text to the same sort of onset. Even so, the conflict always remains internal and between ego and libido. Film and reality participate in the different types of onsets of neurosis, but for the former it is a requirement that there be a neurotic component in order for the subject to become a spectator.

We are resisting the idea that cinema 'causes' neurosis, or that it functions as a milder version of sublimation, in much the same way as psychoanalysis resists the idea that reality 'causes' neurosis. The issue at hand is that what is required to become a *spectator* of a film can best be understood in terms of neurosis, in the taking up of neurosis. Or, to put it another way, the performance of becoming a spectator most closely resembles aspects of the onset of neurosis. (This is not an exclusivity and we shall also be looking towards psychosis and hysteria, amongst others, for further aspects of this idea of becoming spectator). This spectatorial neurosis can be seen as part of the larger order of neurotic illnesses, in as much as it requires a distinction in the mental activities in order to be understood. This, is in part, why the spectator can react as if all that happens on the screen is real, and still make distinctions about its status compared to reality at that moment and later in moments of recalling the film. This issue of reality is crucial to the spectator as neurotic and we should consider this idea a moment longer.

'Preserving error in the heart of reality'

It would seem that reality has a number of functions within the various plays of neurosis. The two that we have been most directly concerned with so far are the causal aspects (that is, the intervention of reality in phantasy causing, for example, frustration) and the comparative. This second function relates to the ways in which we might measure the elements of reality against the neurotic acts. It would be better to think of this as a series of interconnected loops, with notional concepts of reality and phantasy providing the extremes. For this we can adapt Lacan's Rings of Strings and his discussion of Borromean knots.[33] The string we are dealing with here locates reality, phantasy and their filmic moments within a context of neurosis. Given this Lacanian inflection of things here, we can make one further note regarding the notion of the real before proceeding with the model.

It is significant that much of Lacan's thinking about, and formulation of, the real, and what becomes his 'the Real', stems from the influence of Hegel, and Alexandre Kojève's lectures on Hegel. One of the aspects of Kojève's readings that resonates in Lacan's ideas relates to the way in which Hegel transforms the dialectic into a relevance for the real, which in turn has implications for our interests in madness here. Kojève points out that Hegel's reading of the real and the dialectic involves the sense of truth and error. A striking passage is as follows:

> Look at your watch, he [Hegel] says, and note that it is, let us say, noon. Say it, and you will have enunciated a truth. Now write this truth on a piece of paper: 'It is now noon.' At this point Hegel remarks that a truth cannot cease to be true because of being formulated in writing. And now look at your watch again and reread the sentence you have written. You will see that the truth has been transformed into an error, for it is *now* five minutes past noon. What can be said, except that real being can transform a human truth into an error – at least in so far as the real is temporal, and Time has a reality.
>
> (Kojève 1980: 186–7)

Hegel concludes from all this that through his discourse '. . . man succeeds in *preserving* error in the very heart of reality' (Kojève 1980: 187). For Hegel, and within Lacan's echoes, the real/Real becomes the place, for humanity, where error contests the truth. We can read this here as one of the processes, and defining features, of madness. This is the site where that which was once taken as truth now becomes error; that which was once taken for knowledge becomes madness, and vice versa.[34] This relationship is fundamental to Lacan's formulation of the Real, and has significant implications for our concerns with cinema and madness. Once cinema is introduced into this sequence (from the real to error, truth to falsehood, the known to madness) there are considerably more issues involved.

Figure 3.1 illustrates the movement from reality to a site that is composed of film reality. This is the moment where the connection between the film and the ontological order we recognise as reality is strongly maintained. This should not be read simply as mimesis, or even as orders of Realism. It is quite possible to locate the most surreal of films within this site. Indeed, something like *Un chien andalou* or *La jetée* (Marker 1962) can be positioned within this site without any difficulty. For it is not the quality of Realism (which will include the broad sweep from a film's historical accuracy to the ways in which a film adheres to the orthodoxy of realist conventions) that is invested here, rather it is the formation of the spectator's relationship between psychical reality, reality and film's reality (which will also include that particular film being viewed at that moment). The interruption to this is the spectator's recognition of the quasi-real status of the film. Here is an object that feigns reality so well that it traps us in a special type of realist relationship. This is the Hegelian notion of truth and error in the real. When we are spectators of a film it can stand as truth/the real, only becoming 'error' (that is, a filmic reality) afterwards.[35] As with Hegel's example of the watch at noon, the film is true (in many ways it is more true that the true, more real than the real) at that moment of being watched. At the same time the spectator is constantly being reminded (by the film, the viewing context, his/her own viewing habits, other people, and so forth) that this is, after all, only a film. The arc back towards reality, which is produced by such reminders, is caught by the most powerful of forces within the text – that of film phantasy. Once more this has little to do with the phantastic qualities of the actual film text, and we can comfortably, perhaps sometimes necessarily, position a documentary in this site. This film phantasy has more to do with desire, the *objet petit a*, and neurosis. It is also a foundational aspect of what it is to become a cinematic spectator.

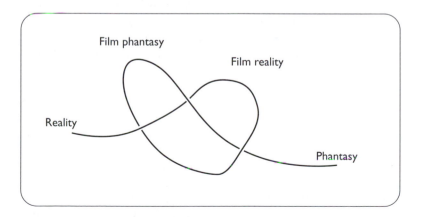

Figure 3.1   Movements of reality and phantasy in film

Film phantasy operates in terms of desire at a number of different levels. There is the easily recognisable (yet analytically complex) level of the production of signs of desire for and by the spectator. This is the multitude of signs that film presents up to us as desirable, as well as those signs the spectator will construct and claim as their own desires. At another level, and one certainly connected to this production, is the idea that these desires are less textually driven and derived, and more a part of the formation of the subject position/type we have designated as the spectator. That is, the spectator cannot exist within the formation of these sorts of desires without there being some form of a configuration of otherness. This is where we discover desire, the *objet petit a*, and neurosis coming into play. We are what we desire because what we desire is an *objet petit a*. This impossible object (of desire) is required to fulfill an impossible function, as Lacan puts it: 'the object that could satisfy *jouissance*' (Lacan 1998: 126). From this interplay emerges neurosis as we must contend with our subjectivity being constructed and confirmed by the Other. This idea can be worked through more fully if we recall Lacan's metaphors of the string and knots.

This very long and sometimes bizarre episode in Lacan's work is revisiting so many of the ideas that had concerned him for many years.[36] In many ways the seminar *Encore* is an attempt to bring together this profound issue of the subject's desire formulated through the Other. Fundamental to this revision are two interconnected points: '*Il semble que le sujet se représente les objets inanimés en fonction de ceci qu'il n'y a pas de relation sexuelle*' (Lacan 1975: 114) (It seems that the subject represents/imagines inanimate objects in the function that there's no such thing as a sexual relation); '*il n'y a pas de sujet connaissant*' (Lacan 1975: 114) (there is no such thing as a knowing subject).[37] From this Lacan proposes that these objects of desire are *a-sexué* (Lacan 1975: 115) – *a*-sexual (in effect bound up to a desire that is both sexualised and beyond the cultural order of sexuality). If this is the case, and subjects lack knowledge and imagine sexual relations, what fills up such lacks? The answer would seem to be the great motifs of Lacan's work (and psychoanalysis) – desire, speech, and the Other. To this we add, via the theories of the gaze, the spectator and his/her scopic drives. These are the moments when meanings are inscribed in certain forms, and where resistances to meaning itself can be seen.

It is perhaps no coincidence that Lacan spends so much of this seminar, on knowledge and love, speaking of strings and knots. To follow this thread further, we can note the idea of knots, solutions and impossibilities. One of the fundamental concepts in Freud's work on the patient's (and unconscious') resistance to analysis is the knot that cannot be disentangled. For Derrida this has even wider implications, having a resonance within the history of western thought. As he puts it:

> there is the tireless insistence [by Freud] on the texture of interwoven threads, on a skein of knots that cannot be untangled. . . . The density of this rhetoric of thread and knot interests us because it appeals to and challenges analysis as a methodical operation of unknotting and technique of untying. It is all a matter of knowing how to pull threads.
>
> (Derrida 1998: 14; 15)

(This is a theme we shall take up once more in Chapter six).

It is this continual process of dreaming up a world full of knowledge, with a plenitude of answers, and relations that are complete, that contributes to the formation of the subject through the Other.[38] And it is because of such relations that we become joined (to ourselves, to others, and to otherness itself) in what Lacan describes as the *échelle des êtres* (the chain of being). Here, then, is the metaphor of the string and knots, for it is important to note that this is one, continuous piece of string. This returns us to the point from which we departed a moment ago. The loop from film reality to film phantasy follows a trajectory towards phantasy itself – which can been seen to contain all these elements of the dream of full knowledge, sexual relations, the repository of the *a*-sexual, the Other, and perhaps even this impossible satisfaction of *jouissance*. Following such a trajectory, however, requires the imposition of neurosis for it leads us beyond the domain of the Symbolic, which almost inevitably must contain the registers of realisms. The cinematic apparatus is formulated through the loops, but never arrives at the extreme end. For if it did it would cease to be cinema as we know it. Perhaps this is cinema's own impossible dream – and one that would take it closer to a type of (representational) madness that would render it unrecognisable to the spectator.

All of this talk of reality, and the formation of truth and error, leads us to one of Freud's fundamental attributes of neurosis, particularly in comparison to psychosis. It is worth recalling that both neurosis and psychosis differ in their primary reactions to the traumatic event, but are remarkably similar in the attempts at expiation. Freud, in relation to this, states: 'Both neurosis and psychosis are thus the expression of a rebellion on the part of the id against the external world, of its unwillingness – or, if one prefers, its incapacity – to adapt to the exigencies of reality' (Freud 1987: 223). The outcomes to this are that neurosis attempts to avoid or ignore reality, whereas psychosis disavows it and creates alternatives to it.[39] Either way, one of the most significant aspects of all this is that the subject's desires are attached to a world of phantasy. Freud argues that this world is 'separated from the real, external world at the time of the introduction of the reality principle' and 'it is from this world of phantasy that the neurosis draws the material for its new wishful constructions' (Freud 1987: 225; 226). Once more, the difference between neurosis and psychosis in this aspect of phantasy is important. Neurosis, Freud argues, will be attached to a part of a reality. This means it can enjoy a status neither strictly in the world of phantasy nor reality, but a combination of the two.

Such a status has a number of important implications for the neurotic spectator and the idea of cinema as neurosis. The cinematic text is always positioned precisely as a part of a world of phantasy attached to a part of reality; and the reality principle is used by the spectator to demarcate the pleasures and travails of watching a film beyond, and within, a sense of reality. The sense of neurosis comes not simply from these relational contexts of phantasy and reality, however. The neurotic spectator is not just enveloping phantasies in senses of realism (and vice versa), but is actually creating substitutes for reality through the attachment of one world order to the other. To do so requires a disturbance beyond the idea of film as a fictional world order. Such an idea insists on the condition that all spectators exist *in potentia* neurotic, and the pleasure of cinema is the continual capacity to construct narratives of neurosis. In other words, it is never a straightforward repetition of the pleasures of escapist phantasies, but rather the pleasure is derived from exploring (largely in an unconscious fashion) the different ways to attach phantasy to reality. Thus the compulsion of this repetition is the mechanism of constructing attachments, rather than the attachments themselves. This is why the neurotic spectator may never be concerned with working out a particular type of neurosis – and so cinema is not a type of therapy – but instead is using the scopic drive to construct a subjectivity that plays with what it is to be neurotic.

A visit to the butchers

I want to close this section with two examples about visits to the butchers, and in doing so head towards the next section that will take up in more detail the idea of the psychotic spectator. The first visit to the butcher is the famous example Freud uses, in *The Interpretation of Dreams* (1985), to show how dreams that are filled with frustration and inconclusion can still be considered wish fulfillments. Here, it is the butcher's wife who dreams of throwing a dinner party but has only a little smoked salmon in the cupboard and all the shops are shut. Thus, she must give up the planned party. Freud's reading of this depends on the woman's jealousy and insecurity regarding her husband, the butcher, and a female friend of theirs. The butcher loves his women large ('Fortunately this friend of hers is very skinny and thin and her husband admires a plumper figure' (Freud 1985: 230). The woman had asked when she was to be invited for another meal, so she could gain some weight. Freud reads this as part of the wish fulfillment of the dream: the party cannot be held because there is no food, the friend cannot gain weight, her marriage to the butcher is safe. And so Freud demonstrates not simply the idea that dreams can contain oppositional meanings to what is being presented, but that there is a level of pleasure within this opposition that can be achieved without any sense of guilt. What Freud is testing is the relationship between the dream and reality, and the pleasures of subversion and seeming unpleasure.

The second visit to the butchers comes from Lacan, who recounts an incident from one of his patients who suffers from *délire à deux* (two people – in this case a mother and daughter – and the same delusion) (see Lacan 1993: 47–56). This woman describes a scene where she passes a man in a corridor that she dislikes (mostly because of his loose morals and ill manners) and complains to Lacan that he said something to her that was very degrading. On being cajoled by Lacan the woman confesses that she was also part of the exchange, muttering to the man 'I've just been to the butcher's'. It is significant to Lacan that she adopts this more elaborate way of saying 'Pig' to the man because it plays into the system of hallucination and coded discourse. The man's response to this is to say 'Sow!'

What is of perhaps greater significance here is Lacan's brief comment on understanding and meaning. He prefaces his elaboration on the statement 'I've just been to the butcher's' with the idea that we recognise something to be understood through delusion: 'The important thing is not to understand, but to attain the true. . . . Naturally, I understand – which proves that we all have a little something in common with delusionals. I have within myself, as you have within yourselves, what there is that is delusional in the normal man' (Lacan 1993: 48). From this we mark a moment that is a recurring motif in this discussion – that cinema declares itself as something to be understood and to have meaning, yet it must also constantly assert its status of delusion. And like the dream of the butcher's wife, cinema's meanings are premised on a multitude, some in conflict with each other, sometimes in contrast with what has been defined as pleasurable.

Understanding in cinema, like the woman's statement of visiting the butcher, is recognised not because it is founded on truth and reality, but because it is founded on a type of delusion that demands to be considered as something to be understood. The seemingly incoherent exchange of a visit to the butcher and 'Sow!' makes it something in the order of understanding as well as what Lacan describes as 'a rupture in the system of language' (Lacan 1993: 55). What is meant may not be clear, may indeed be unresolvable, but it continues to assert its status as meaningful. Cinema is of this same order of rupture in the Symbolic and its language system(s), and in order for this rupture to exist the cinematic spectator must be formed. This is fundamentally tied to the issue of knowledge, meaning and the cinema spectator, but before we can engage with this we must consider a more extreme version of the spectator. This will take us to the place of psychosis.

CHAPTER 4

The Psychotic Spectator who Transgresses

The previous chapter signaled some of the ways in which neurosis and psychosis establish, and operate, different sorts of relationships to reality. This allowed us to mark some of the differences between these two orders in terms of the representational fields of madness as well as the act of cinema spectatorship. The following section continues these ideas, pursuing this time psychosis and cinema. The first part of the chapter will look at the difficulties of psychosis and language, and how psychoanalysis has positioned this as one of the key defining aspects. This, in turn, will allow us to compare the language of the psychotic to different aspects of cinema. One of the key aspects to be considered will be the ways in which the spectator 'adopts' a type of psychotic language in order to watch a film. This will include the idea of cinematic language as a type of disturbance. The final section of the chapter will examine hallucination in psychosis and how cinema can be seen to perform a similar process.

It must be stated at the outset that the ideas in this chapter are complicated by the nature of what is being dealt with. In some ways psychosis is the least penetrable of the psychical disturbances. The level of resistance to understanding and interpretation make it difficult, sometimes impossible, to explicate. To a certain extent this is all the more reason to engage in it. Yet we will be confronted at almost every turn with the sense that to use psychosis to understand the cinematic spectator is a genuine challenge. What lies at the heart of psychosis is a fundamental aspect of the spectator's relationship to cinema.

There is something altogether more extreme, more forceful about psychosis; it is for Lacan madness itself[40], and its history is marked by the constant struggles to define it, as well as its resistances to such definitions. Psychoses threaten because they resist – not just these analytic acts of definition, nor just the historical pursuits of knowing them, but the very notions of representation, containment, and understanding. There is always something that approaches the psychotic in all acts of resistance, all acts that confound meaning and explication. This is partly its seductive quality – although this is a seduction caught once more in that threat of disempowerment and the risk of silence found in all acts of madness – that allows a spirit of resistance. The three aspects of cinema that have been central to this study – the problematics of representing the mad act, the cinematic apparatus as an incitement to madness, and the cinematic spectator as he/she partakes in an act of madness – are enveloped in the processes of psychoses. And, because of this, all find themselves beyond reason and order and almost necessarily as potential sites of resistance. These are our recurring motifs: how can something like psychoses be represented (and how are we to recognise and read such signs)? How is cinema itself like psychoses? And how does the act of becoming a film spectator compare to a psychotic episode? The artifice of separating these three issues sometimes serves us well, and other times it hinders progress. Here we shall avoid separation – handling psychoses is difficult enough without presenting more issues of division. Instead, we shall proceed through a number of themes and concepts that are central to the idea of psychosis and its cinematic relations.

On the bed: the language of the psychotic

It is not only psychoanalysis that has struggled with the idea of a language of psychoses. If we take the line – perhaps too generous a line it is granted – that psychoses are found in all acts of resistance to meaning, then any system that attempts to articulate the processes of meaning in language systems has, at some point, needed to confront this issue of the seeming non-meaning of certain signs and constructions.[41] Be it a linguistic analysis of a political speech, geometrical formulae for the analysis of space, the biological reading of swarming ants, rules on perspective in painting, the instruction manual for assembling a bed – all have emerged from a process that at some point has attempted to exclude the impossible, the destruction of meaning, the limits of knowledge. This is the task such systems set themselves – to map the signifier's relationship to the signified so that a transparency of meaning exists. Yet, what haunts them all is this shadow of misreadings and aberrant decodings. Furthermore, it is not simply a single code we engage in even with the most simple of examples; and each layering of codes marks a point for the possible insertion of a breakdown in the language, of an unhinging of the signifier/signified order of things – that is, psychoses.

This cleaving of the sign is what constitutes the onset of psychosis for Lacan. It is the moment when the sign is divided into its constitutive elements of signifier and signified (see, for example, Lacan 1993: 268) so that it cannot function in quite the same manner. A bed is assembled according to instructions, made up with linen and pillows, placed centrally in the room and next to a wall – this is the bed of the Symbolic order, where the sign is held together by considerations of design, function, and even aesthetics. But the psychotic's bed can be manifested at any number of levels that causes it to be a site of resistance to the Symbolic bed. It is not just the dysfunctionally assembled bed that marks the psychoses, but its uses, positions, histories, and images that can convey this. The breakdown of the sign can take place at any number of different levels, and in any number of different articulations. This is part of the creativity of psychosis, for it presents ruptures and fissures in the most unusual of conditions.

This is why we can take this issue at two different levels – that of the spectator and that of the representation of psychosis. For example, beds with restraints on the railing mark sexual play as well as psychoses: *Basic Instinct* (Verhoeven 1992) has the bed of the murderously sexual; *The Cell* (Singh 2000) has the bed with elaborate chains that allows the serial killer to be agonisingly, yet ecstatically, suspended above his victim. This is the 'primitive' bed of the madman which is visually different from the hi-tech bed of the laboratory that allows Catherine Deane to enter the unconscious of another, and yet serves precisely the same function (the manifestation of the unconscious to the other); *Tie Me Up, Tie Me Down* (Almodóvar 1990) has the bed of sexual imprisonment masquerading as desire and love; the marriage bed in *That Obscure Object of Desire* (Buñuel 1977) is part of the obscurity of desire, for each time the sheets are pulled back it is unclear how, or even if, desires will be satisfied. Such beds are part of the Symbolic (they still have a certain aspect of 'bedness' about them, we recognise the features of a bed, we confirm these functions, and so forth)

and yet are also part of a psychotic sign system, forming a paradigm of signs that cinema utilises to convey madness.

The problem here, of course, is that cinema (as a Symbolic
process) is constructing an artifice of psychotic language precisely
to convey madness and excess. As soon as we see some form of
restraint (handcuffs, chains, strapping, as well as the emotional
such as in *That Obscure Object of Desire* or the beginning and end
scenes of *Belle de jour* (Buñuel 1967)) we slip into the repository of
cinematic signs that connote (potential) acts of madness and
excess. The irony being that through this system of representation,
cinema has transformed the split sign of psychosis into a closely
integrated one. The psychoses are positioned into a schema that
makes them recognisable, makes them readable, and gives meaning (in that they now mean 'this is psychosis/madness'). Or, at
least this is true at one level. We may see the contraption that is a
bed for the serial killer in *The Cell* and recognise the cinematic
signs that insists on 'madness', but in doing so what we really see is
a highly conventionalised form. This is not a psychotic's bed – this
is the psychotic's bed seen from the Symbolic via the cinematic.
And yet perhaps this is precisely how it must be. Only the psychotic
can make his/her own bed, see it for what it is, and everything else
is re-presentation.

This struggle with reading, recognising, and even reproducing
the language of psychosis is undoubtedly a significant one.
However, there is another aspect to this that removes some of the
difficulties of resolving the seeming impossibilities of glissading
inherently oppositional language systems into one another. That
is, the highly codified languages of the Symbolic that constantly
demand the complete sign, and the resistant languages of madness
that split the signifier from its signifieds.[42] This is the idea that
cinema is a language that occupies both the discourse of the rational, of reality (in effect the Symbolic), and of madness, and what it
requires from its spectator is the capacity to constantly move
between both forms.

Cinematic language is Symbolic inasmuch as it operates culturally and has established systems that enable it to be read. However,
our argument here is that this language is also closely linked to
madness, and the cinematic experience requires certain acts of
simulated madness in order to work. Or, perhaps more accurately,
to become the cinematic spectator requires an experience far
more like acts of madness (such as psychosis) than any other

system of thought. In short, what constitutes a certain, and primary, feature of cinema is madness. The filmed version of a psychotic's bed is highly Symbolic, but by being looked at by the *becoming cinematic spectator*, this bed is also located as a type of madness. (We use 'becoming' here because the spectator is in a constant state of emerging and never fully arrives. This is because cinema itself never really arrives and no spectator's relationship to it is fixed). In this sense, any bed in a film is subject to a variation of madness (it has already been framed at the very least by the mad acts of watching a film) – the psychotic's bed is a further demarcation within this system. This can be illustrated by pushing the example further. The hospital bed, with its white, crisp, sterile sheets and pillow, coupled with the restraints, is the psychotic's bed as delivered up in the Symbolic. This is the bed for the psychotic, as distinct from the bed by the psychotic – yet both are the psychotic's bed. The hospital bed is recognised by the spectator as a cultural construction, whereas the bed in which the psychotic performs his/her acts is to be recognised as a construction from the psychosis. Of course, both beds emerge from a cultural construction; the difference is that one declares this in order to have its meaning asserted, whereas the other denies it for precisely the same reasons.

Perhaps this example is less randomly chosen than might originally seem to be the case. After all, the bed is a site of the great Freudian themes – sex, dreams, and more often than not in the cinematic mad person, death. It is also, by association, linked with the processes of analysis. It is an image of extreme intimacy made impersonal, and so operates very much within the liminal space of the mainstream social order and private existences. It is the bed, or at least the bedroom, which carries many of the images of the mad in cinema. The most famous scene in *Psycho* (Hitchcock 1960), for example, may well be the stabbing in the shower, but the sequence begins and ends in the bedroom. These framing shots of the bedroom contextualise the acts of violence, voyeurism, sexuality, Marion's betrayal, and so on and operate as a private space (for Marion), a voyeuristic space (for Norman), and a psychotic space for Norman/Mother. It is significant that the film opens with a shot that penetrates the window of a hotel bedroom, signaling infidelity, immorality and deceit. These are resistances to monogamy and the family that are often seen as acts of madness. For all the madness of

Norman, many of Marion's acts can also be seen as slippages into madness as well.

It is this curious mix, then, of the social and intimate, the public and the private, that allows the sliding between the language of the Symbolic and the languages of psychoses. It is also what allows for a merging of the Symbolic with the Imaginary, especially in terms of psychoses, where the Imaginary is highly significant. The spectator may recognise the bedroom as a cultural construction, note its parallels to his/her own bedroom, derive a sense/meaning of it from the repository of bedrooms that are available to them. And yet the spectator can always have the framing reference that here is the source of voyeuristic delights and transgressions. Thus, the bedroom scenes in cinema immediately work within a sense of exceeding the social domain.

We are not very far from Lacan's seminar on psychoses here. In mapping out the upcoming sessions in this seminar, he points out that the overall aim is to locate psychosis in terms of the orders of the Imaginary, the Symbolic and the Real; this is a seminar that will prove vital to our working through psychoses and cinema. For what Lacan sees as psychoanalysis' struggle with psychoses, we can see as cinema's psychotic underpinnings. And it is Lacan who can provide us with a way forward in regard to this issue of cinema as a language of psychosis in the spectator.

Soul murder and calibene: Schreber and Rivière

Before we proceed it is worth noting how psychoanalysis has attempted to come to terms with the literal manifestation of the language of psychoses. For, in this, we observe that psychoanalysis sets itself the task of reading psychosis, because in it lies not just answers to madness, but also how the unconscious operates for everyone. One of the most famous studies of this sort of material is Judge Schreber; less famous, but also of significance here, is the case of Pierre Rivière.[43] From this we can proceed to the psychotic cinematic relationships of representation and spectatorship.

The case of Rivière contains many rich elements, but there are two that are of immediate relevance here. The first is that we see throughout the articulate and poetic account of his acts and deeds, Rivière's need to invent words for items he devises and actions he commits. What is striking about these neologisms is that they are very much part of himself. There is a passage, for example, where Rivière talks about becoming famous and being well liked by others (set within a context of enacting revenge on those who have been cruel to him). Part of the way in which he thinks he can do this is by creating new instruments: 'I resolved first to make a tool to kill birds such as had never before been seen, I named it "calibene"' (Foucault 1975: 103). Similarly, he made bows for his children friends that he called 'albalesters'. He also had names for various acts: 'I crucified frogs and birds, I had also invented another torture to put them to death. It was to attach them to a tree with three sharp nails through the belly. I called that enceepharating them' (Foucault 1982: 104). So these are words not just for new acts, but acts and ideas from Rivière himself – they come to represent his subjectivity to himself, and for everyone else. And because they have this representation of the self, this highly self-reflexive modality, they become a further indication of his madness. Yet these are not ordinary utterances of madness (if there can ever be such a thing), but are located within such a highly codified language system that they declare meaningfulness. These are the sites of translated madness by the psychotic. This is the same for Schreber's invented discourse, particularly the phrase *Seelenmord* (soul murder) which the psychotic himself sees as a powerful word that exists outside the Symbolic domain.

The other issue that emerges from Rivière's memoirs is the motivation for the brutal killings. There appear to be three, although Rivière does not speak of them as such. The first is the family history that Rivière recounts – one of unhappiness between his father (whom he adored) and his mother and the sense that Rivière believed his father to be so very badly mistreated. The account is full of seemingly minor anecdotes (such as the father going hungry because the mother would not kiss him at a meal), which accumulate into what Rivière perceives as a totally repressive situation. The second motivation comes from Rivière's readings of books. At one point he states that he had read in Roman history the rights of the husband to kill his wife and children. Similarly, when he attempts to formulate (and justify) his actions of killing most of his family, Rivière refers to a book on the history of shipwrecks and the sacrificing of crew members so others could survive. Such a sacrifice, he figures, is what he must commit for his father.[44] Finally, Rivière says that he was carrying out the will of God. As he constantly states: 'God inspired me, he ordered me to do it, I obeyed his orders, and he is protecting me' (Foucault 1982: 121). And yet Rivière himself admits that this is something that runs counter to the other motivations (especially what he saw as the need to avenge his father) and he speaks of repenting, of needing to speak the truth, and of the heavy weight this defence (of God) has given him. Finally, we find a powerful sexual current running through Rivière's memoirs – kissing, for example, carries extraordinary force in terms of acceptance, rejection, and formations of subjectivity.

Similarly, Schreber's interpretation of the world, and all the things done to him, are contextualised within a sexual dynamic (including homosexuality and trans-sexuality), a family history (including Schreber's ideas on creating his own family), and the intervention of ideas from books and reading. Sexual relations, in particular, become the core of the hermeneutic act in reading the actions of the mad. Another example of this is the Papin sisters who murdered their employer and her daughter in 1933. The crime seemed to be shocking not just because of its brutality (both women were bashed with an iron, had their eyes gouged out, and hacked with kitchen utensils) but also because the sisters had an incestuous, sexual relationship. The film version, *Sister, My Sister* (Meckler 1994) captures the alienation of the sisters, the brutality of their existence, and the seemingly inevitable collapse into madness. It did not show the life of the two sisters after the court hearings, with Christine (the eldest and main instigator of the murders) dying in prison. Her anguish must have been intense during this time: 'Christine suffered from fainting spells and hallucinations. She would try to gouge out her own eyes, spread her arms as though on a cross, and indulge in sexual exhibitionism' (Roudinesco 1997: 63). And in all of this we find the same recurring themes and acts.

These four motivations – family histories, the influence of reading, a religious force, and sexual acts – are very common in the literatures of, and on, the mad from the eighteenth century onwards, and they are very strong images within the cinematic representation of the mad. It would be inaccurate to argue that all four are always present, or that they have equal intensity, but as recurring motifs they appear with considerable regularity. This is not just the more literal versions, such as is found in *Sister, My Sister*, but also in less readily apparent, perhaps even less psychotic versions. One such example is *American Beauty* (Mendes 1999), where the psychoses are more diffuse and much less extreme than in the words of Schreber and Rivière, yet demonstrate very similar traits. So much of the dysfunction stems from family breakdown and the desire to recreate new families. Just as the Papin sisters, Schreber and Rivière desire to purge one family in order to create a new one (and, with the latter two particularly, seeing themselves as the one who gives 'birth' to this new order) so we find different people attempting the creation of a different order, including Lester's return to a lost youth. (The same sorts of motivations are found in other films, such as Travis Bickle's new family order, Norman Bates as the mother, and so forth).

Psychotic acts, such as Lester Burnham's attempted escape to youth and Colonel Fitts' shooting of him, are also mapped out within sexual contexts. Even the versions of psychoses seen in Angela Hayes (the false identity of sexual prowess and experience), Lester's daughter, Jane, (exhibitionism), and Ricky Fitts (scopophilia, voyeurism) have sexual origins and force. Each of these acts also contains disavowal of certain attributes that in reality (their Symbolic world) actually defines each of them. Within all these representations of psychosis is the spectator's experience of his/her own variation on this. This is most overtly shown when the film sets up a collusion between what is shown as if it is taking place and Lester's phantasising. The scene where he imagines kissing Angela in the kitchen is revealed to be just that – imaginary. However, the spectator is shown this only after they have been 'tricked' into thinking that the kiss has taken place. It is revealed to be a phantasy the moment Lester pulls a rose petal from his mouth, in part because of the impossibility of the petal, and in part because roses have already been established as part of his phantasising. But until that moment it is as real for him as it is for the spectator.

A different sort of example is *Walkabout* (Roeg 1971), where there is a type of culturally-derived interpretation of madness. The murderous attempts (by shooting and abandoning his children in the desert), and suicide, of the father come across as a form of madness which are paralleled by the Aboriginal's own suicide at the close of the film. Between them is a sort of idyllic reinvention of the family where desert gives way to a dream-like plenitude of water and fruit. (A version that feeds into the contrast of a spiritually moribund city and the threat to the Dream-time spirituality of the Aboriginal people). The actions of both the father and the

Aboriginal are seen as a type of madness by the girl. These acts, caught up in versions of sexuality and death, seem to exclude the young boy and pass unobserved by him.

It would be over simplifying, however, to argue that these four processes are the primary formation and constitution of a psychotic language – and that all signs of psychosis will contain such elements. At the very least such a summary carries with it the mistake of not acknowledging the template of the discourse of madness that has necessarily been placed on all such cases. In other words, we may see a set of recurring themes (such as the family, sexuality, religion and the seductive forces of transgression that the text holds for the spectator), but at the same time we must recognise the discourses that encase and interpret (through predisposition), them. This is precisely Foucault's project in the collection of the medical and legal documents that surround the Rivière memoirs; it is also part of the radical rereading that Lacan gives the Papin sisters case when he looks to the socio-psychical forces at play; and it is the interpretative gesture that Freud makes when he reads Schreber's memoirs. And yet these commentators become part of the very discourse they are attempting to analyse. This is all part of the language of psychosis – it is the moment where all discourses meet, from the psychotic's invention of signs to the attempts to read them outside of the context in which they are generated. Positioned in this way the psychotic becomes the site of resistance for the sorts of things Foucault aligns to 'statements' (see, for example, Foucault 1970). Let us now return to the idea of the image, for this is where we find a key aspect of the psychotic in the cinematic Imaginary.

Psychotic disturbances of the cinematic language

What we have termed the cinematic Imaginary – the relationship between the becoming spectator and the cinematic – is essential to these issues of the discourses of the psychoses. It is part of what Lacan describes as the 'order of relations of understanding' (Lacan 1993: 9) between the subject and his/her world order. For our concerns here, this must at the very least constitute how the spectator comes to terms with the representation of madness, and how he/she becomes part of that configuration. This is the idea that the becoming spectator is part of the formation of this psychotic language, for it is realised through the gaze of the cinema spectator. This is a parallel that functions at many different levels. To list the ones we have so far: the psychotic's own language read through its particular discourses (the *Seelenmord* of Schreber, the *enceepharating* of Rivière, the self-mutilation of Christine Papin, and so forth); the cinematic 'translation' of these signs into narrative representations (such as Lester Burnham, Colonel Fitts, Norman Bates, at the level of characterisation, as well as specific moments, such as the rose petal in the mouth as a blurring of phantasy and reality); the discourses that attempt to analyse them (such as psychoanalysis, history, science and medicine, as well as the cinematic apparatus).

To this (incomplete) list we can add the spectator's mirroring of the psychoses in order to watch a film. This complex relationship operates in itself at a number of different levels. If in no other way, and at the very least, the spectator is like the psychotic because of the paranoia involved in reading a film. Just as when we watch a film all elements have the possibility of meaning, so too does the psychotic interpret the world. Lacan argues the psychotic finds him/herself as a foreigner in the world, and as such finds meaningfulness in every act and object, every event and moment. The psychotic feels a constant gaze upon themselves, not just from other people, but from literally everything. It is not simply other people who seem to spy on the psychotic but the non-human objects of the world. (See for example, Lacan 1993: 9 where this sense of being spied on by the world itself is sometimes even seen as a wink). This can work as part of our definition of the cinema spectator – one who sees everything as a sign, and who feels the entire world of the film is addressed towards him/herself. Not only that, but objects do have a gaze and a speech that is directed at the spectator of the film. The close-up of the star thrown into the dust at the end of *High Noon* (Zinnemann 1952) gives that inanimate object the capacity to speak to, point, look, and yes even wink at the spectator. Of course it does not do this solely by itself, but in combination with the required acts of spectating in order to attribute meaning to the badge.

Of course, as we have noted elsewhere, it is not enough, even at the level of metaphor, to conflate the acts of madness with the processes of the spectator because they can be seen to demonstrate certain shared traits. Our struggle here is with the impossibilities of madness and the fecund nature of spectatorship; of how each of these operates in excess to any critical and interpretive configuration or representational attempt. So let us continue with this line, establishing some further points of connection, before returning to the issue of representation and the language of the psychotic. This, in turn, will lead us to the idea that delusions and hallucinations operate in a comparable fashion for the psychotic and the cinema spectator.

For psychoanalysis, one of the essential features of psychosis is the disruption of language, and in Lacan we find a sustained analysis of precisely this disturbed relationship between the psychotic and the signifier. 'Language' can be taken, quite legitimately, in a much broader sense than spoken or written language. The body is the hysteric's language, for example. In this spirit, we can make connections to cinematic language in these terms. Lacan is clear that the recognition and interpretation of psychosis depends on the analyst's capacity to identify certain language disturbances.[45]

This is a crucial point – Lacan does not append the issue of language to psychosis, for him, the two are the same issue. One cannot even see the psychotic, cannot recognise that which is psychosis without reference to language. The problem for our concerns here is how such disruptions are to be recognised within the cinematic signifiers (and the whole spread of issues from this, such as the language of the visual). This is not the cataloguing of the types of disturbances, but rather aligning the disturbances of psychosis with the act of spectating. Such a distinction is necessary here because what is at hand is not the idea that the film text simply represents, or even replicates, psychopathologies, but that the act of spectating requires us to accept, experience, and/or construct language disturbances, and so act in a psychotic manner.

The key to this is that if we, as spectators of a film, *understand* the language of the film we are entering into a complex range of disturbances. These disturbances are instigated at the level of language, but operate across the entire range of the cinematic experience. The created world order of the film text, which necessarily functions with such certainty, sets up disturbances to the spectator. It must do this or the very pleasures and erotics of watching a film would never take place. The initial disturbance is entering into the created world order of a particular film and engaging in the elements within it. In order for this to be possible some form of psychosis must take place. After this, we follow the psychotic's lead, allowing images, ideas and emotions to be real; when we shed tears at a tragic moment or recoil in fear at a frightening one, we are allowing the disturbances of the Symbolic language that cinema is to perform as, that is stand in for, reality. This is the becoming spectator of cinema, using the invented images (like the invented words of the psychotic) to have powerful meanings and certainty. For, in those moments, the images are the reality and the certainty of the psychotic spectator.

As we have noted elsewhere, the spectator eroticises the signifier in order to develop a relationship with it. We can now add further to this point. The psychotic has a particular relationship to the signifier. It is one based on an alienated position that the psychotic finds him/herself in as they shift from the world of their madness into the Symbolic (and vice versa). This is the phenomena of 'making sense' of the disturbances, as well as the world in which they are now located. Rivière's invented signifiers refer to acts and objects within the world, just as Schreber's complex belief structure attempts to make sense of the world as he sees it through his psychosis. The spectator is placed in a comparable position. When an event takes place in a film, the spectator must read the invented signifiers so that they make sense, even if outside of the film they would be quite irrational or make very little sense. However, this process goes beyond the need to read the signs within the filmic world order; what is also taking place is a positioning of the spectator within those inventions. When we are spectators of a film we more than simply watch – we include our own psychic processes through the invention of the signifiers themselves.

When Lacan describes the psychotic as having 'this disadvantage, but also this privilege, of finding himself a little at odds with, askew in relation to, the signifier' (Lacan 1993: 322) we can track similar relationships with the spectator when they watch a film. The relationships between the signifier of the Symbolic order and the signifier of the film's created world order set up demands that require the spectator to be in this skewed site. Such disturbances relate to the ways in which the language is read. In other words, these are not necessarily signifiers never before seen, rather it is a new position for seeing all signs. The psychotic and the spectator occupy sites that require them to reassess their relationship to language (in the broadest sense of the term). Furthermore, this is the place where meanings are sought and established after negating the other sites of meaning, and signifiers of pure phantasy demand to be seen as real; false objects and events acquire the status of reality.

Here we come up against the issue of understanding, and there are at least two ways of tracking this. Firstly, there is the most easily recognised notion – of how things are understood. Secondly, there is the issue of how something attains the status of understandability. These two are not, of course, always totally distinct, but the spectator as psychotic reveals just how significant the second, in particular, can be in forming meaning within the cinema. What is being argued here is that the cinematic signifier acquires the status of understandability in much the same way that the signifier of madness does. Or, put another way, the spectator generates meaning from the web of cinematic signifiers – that is, gives them understandability – in a manner comparable to acts of psychosis. This is not, it should be pointed out, the act of interpretation, rather it is the recognition of a sign within its context as understandable.

An example will help illustrate this. The invention of words by the psychotic to represent his/her world (which, as noted above, is also a representation of the self within a new relationship to the sign) is like the jump-cut when it first appeared in the films of the French New Wave. By going against the established Symbolic language of montage, the jump-cut disrupts the language of film. The spectator, however, can attribute understanding to the jump-cut both within the context of editing and narrative, and the rule-breaking demands of, for example, Godard's films. In such an example, we find the double inflection of psychosis. The jump-cut disrupts the established language of montage, like a term such as *Seelenmord* or Christine Papin's self-mutilation, disrupts, seems mad, in the rational, everyday world, and so stands for the psychosis. At the same time, the spectator of *A bout de souffle* attributes meaning and understandability to the jump-cut, just as Schreber sees meaning and understandability in his concept of *Seelenmord*. In doing so, the spectator is more like the psychotic who enters this world order (and there understands it), and less like the analyst who attempts to distance him/herself from the created world order (who attempts to interpret it).

It is significant that the meaning of such disturbances function in a very particular manner. Lacan makes a very important point in regards to Schreber's invented words, and to a patient of his own who uses the word *galopiner* which Lacan sees as the summation of her psychosis and paranoia. Lacan argues that these special words function not as meaningful, but in terms of meaning: 'The meaning of these words that pull you up has the property of referring essentially to meaning *as such*. It's a meaning that essentially refers to nothing but itself, that remains irreducible' (Lacan 1993: 33). In these terms, the jump-cut, or even something like the extraordinarily long takes without the expected cuts (such as the battle scene in the French village in *The Longest Day* (Annakin, Morton, Oswald, Wicki 1962) that flows on and on, following the soldiers through the streets and along the river without a break, circling and twisting in on itself), can be seen as referring to meaning itself – in these examples the meaning of editing in narrative cinema, or the meaning of duration in a shot sequence.

This is not to argue that such devices do not have meanings within the films themselves (or even emotional and narrative effect), but as with the invented language of the psychotic, the disturbance initially takes us back to the formations of meaning, and certainly initially they pull us up as spectators of the film. To follow Lacan's example further: 'Before being reducible to another meaning it signifies within itself something ineffable, it's a meaning that refers above all to meaning as such' (Lacan 1993: 33). So too the disturbances of jump-cuts and extra long takes – they do have other, additional meanings, but at first they signify something about meaning in cinema itself.

But where, it must be asked, does this level of understanding operate? It is important to recall that what is taking place in psychosis, just as what is taking place when we become spectators of a film, is a certain insertion and emphasis of the ego, of the subject him/herself. When we follow the discourse of Schreber we find a careful mapping out of the self in relation to the world. It is not simply Scherber's interpretation of the world, it is far more his sense of himself in the world. The entire language structure of the psychosis is based around a making sense of the world through the self's position in it. One of the more overt demonstrations of this is paranoid psychosis, which operates in terms of the formation of the self precisely through the sense of threat.[46] The paranoid subject comes into being, exists, and makes sense of the world, because of the feelings of threat. In doing so they also make that world part of their own, created world order. The same idea can be carried over to the spectator, for during that moment of becoming a spectator of the film the subject's existence resides in the act of watching. This is enacted through the cinematic demands for the insertion of the subject into the created world order. This created world order, we have argued throughout, is directly linked to the psychic reality of the spectator. We can map these relationships in terms of each other and the production of the text – either filmic ones or manifestations of psychoses (see Figure 4.1).

Here we find ourselves back at the issue of the relationship between the psychic reality and the reality of the created world order as they are both differentiated from the reality of the Symbolic order – that which comes to stand for reality itself. As was noted in the previous chapter, Freud's initial working through of the distinction between neurosis and psychosis relied heavily on the relationship between the subject, reality, and psychical reality. Our concern here is how psychical reality might somehow be seen in terms of the created world order (that is, the textual reality) of film. Lacan will, once more, provide us with a way of tackling this complex set of issues.

Lacan's reading of psychosis (which is Freudian in itself) emphasises the role of phantasy and the ways in which the subject utilises these creations to negotiate the world. Let us take a couple

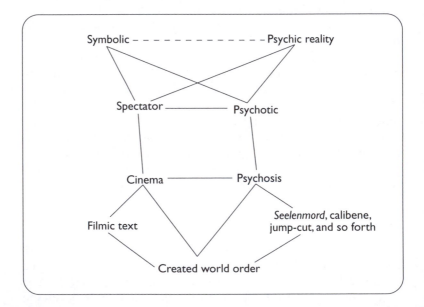

Figure 4.1 **Relationships between the spectator and psychotic in terms of reality**

of significant quotes from his seminars: 'In psychosis. . . reality itself initially contains a hole that the world of phantasy will subsequently fill'; and later: 'Let's start with the idea that a hole, a fault, a point of rupture, in the structure of the external world finds itself patched over by psychotic phantasy' (Lacan 1993: 45). As tempting as it might be, we cannot transpose this too literally onto the act of the spectator. Before we can instigate further ideas at the level of film and psychic reality, we need to consider the relationship of this hole to film as phantasy, as well as the relationship between film to reality.

One of the points we are aiming towards is the idea that the hole, the lack of the signifier, in psychosis operates in a similar way to the lack that a film provides. Note that we say here that a film *provides* the lack, the hole, and not that a film attempts to fill such a (psychotic) hole. The reason for this has to do with the structure of the Other and the ego in the formation of the spectator – but more of this later. The sorts of questions and issues that we are dealing with here include: is film's reality (that is, the created world order in combination with the acts of spectating) part of the patch or part of the hole? What are the relationships between film's phantasy structures and the other orders of reality (psychical and the reality of the world)? What are the connections between film and psychotic phantasies? These are by no means all the questions raised – but they are a start.

Lacan's negotiation of psychoses shows the turn of brilliance that makes him worthwhile. In making the issue one about *Verwerfung* (foreclosure[47]), Lacan moves our understanding in a quite surprising direction. Foreclosure, both Freud and Lacan insist, is quite distinct from repression. Freud's commentary on the Wolf Man (Sergei Pankejeff) case includes the idea that Pankejeff rejects part of reality as if it does not exist. Lacan extends this, arguing that foreclosure also takes place at the level of the unconscious. So the parts of reality that have been rejected (so they do not exist for that subject) are also not part of the repressed material of the unconscious. In this sense it is also rejected from the unconscious. Lacan defines foreclosure as 'what has been placed outside the general symbolization structuring the subject – return from without' (Lacan 1993: 47). (This return from without can be read in the sense of exclusion of this material from the unconscious). It is this particular quality that has a great deal of relevance to the formation and performance of psychoses. What we need to consider now is the ways in which the spectator engages in similar acts of foreclosure in order to watch a film.

A note on foreclosure and the spectator

Let us be clear about this, for it is complex. Foreclosure is not repression, but the disavowal, the rejection and fending off, of a part of reality. In psychoanalysis the hole that is left must be 'filled' so to speak; two possibilities are phantasy and fetishism.[48] There are a number of ways in which this can be seen to be operating in terms of cinema. Firstly, there is the idea that films actually demand a similar act of foreclosure, this time of reality itself. So when we are spectators we effectively disavow reality, allowing the created world order of the film to participate in the formation, as well as simulate a filling in of, the hole left by such an act. Although this might sound comparable to the long-standing idea (in literary theory) of the willing suspension of disbelief, quite the opposite is the case. What is being argued here is that no such suspension ever takes place in any textual reading, and what is posited as disbelief in such a formula, is, like repression, less important than the act of disavowal. When we watch a film, reality (that is, both the everyday as well as the Symbolic) is not repressed, rather it is fended off in order that a different reality (that of the film) can dominate. In this sense, the spectator performs foreclosure in much the same way as the psychotic does. For both subject positions it is embedded in a sense of pleasure and existence in the self.

Secondly, there is a multiplicity of disavowals taking place whenever we watch a film. These are the lacunae of the film that make the whole act of watching a film so pleasurable. Disavowals such as these are more textually driven, deriving their force from the very absences that constitute a film. Such lacunae are essential to any film for they draw the spectator into the text by making him/her a collaborator. Once we, as spectators, start filling in the spots of indeterminacy we become part of the textual order, constructing its pleasures and desires, its acts of seduction and moments of entrapment. To do this requires foreclosure of the real world and an investment (psychic, emotional, intellectual, and so on) in the textual world.

Thirdly, there are the disavowals that take place through the spectator's own histories of foreclosure. This is the spectator 'using' the film to disavow aspects of his/her own reality. This can be anything as simple as the disavowal of the Great Depression through elaborate and excessive displays of wealth in the Hollywood musicals of the 1930s, through to a complex relationship of the spectator's 'acting out', psychically speaking, of the phantasies of the film's created world order. This would seem to side-step the potentially difficult conjecture that cinema can act as a type of foreclosure for the spectator's own issues of the unconscious. However, what is revealed here is that cinema's function is not foreclosure, but rather to perform a duality that may at times seem contradictory. Cinema must, at the same time, create the hole as well as the textual patch on the hole in the phantasy. It is here that we come closest to the heart of the cinematic as psychosis. To follow this through further we can turn to the issues of hallucination.

Hallucination, delusion and phantasy

What is cinema if not hallucination? But it is not any general sense of hallucination that organises and drives cinema, but a very particular type. The issue at hand here is how much cinematic hallucination can be seen to parallel the hallucinations attached to psychosis. For the psychotic, hallucination is a fundamental survival strategy; it is not only part of the disavowal of a piece of reality, it is also the construction of a phantasy that enables the denial to continue and escape to take place. For the psychotic, the hallucination defines his/her relationship to the world and enables them to negotiate the seeming contradictions. One area of potential difficulty in reading cinema and psychosis in terms of hallucination is the very specific nature of the psychotic's hallucinations, as distinct from the culturally (and textually) shared hallucination of cinema.

There are at least three responses to this: firstly, we have already noted the idea that cinema allows for a similar invention of language-specific processes. *Seelenmord* is highly particular to Schreber's psychotic hallucinations, but it can pass into the Symbolic (even if it continually signals its own disjunctive positionings), just as the rose petal passes into the Symbolic of both Lester Burnham and the spectator of the kiss with Angela; films continually invent divergences of their own language (the jump-cut, the steady-cam, shifts in the use of lighting, restructuring narrative devices, for example) that can pass into a wider sense of cinema, but initially operate within a sense of disruption and distortion. Secondly, cinema's social functions rely on a shared sense of experiences, but these are continually read within a context unique to the spectator. The hallucination of heterosexuality as the only sexual order is a social structure that relies on a certain cultural acceptance, but it can still be resisted through a homosexual (especially in terms of Queer theory) politic. Similarly, phallocentrism privileges a certain type of sexuality and gender performance; but it is a hallucination that passes as 'truth' because it is so heavily invested in the layers of the social order. The third, and perhaps the most significant, is that there does not have to be a sense of a chasm between the Symbolic and the psychotic in terms of the hallucination. Lacan precisely defines the hallucinatory phenomenon as 'the subject's history in the Symbolic' (Lacan 1993: 13). In other words, as with cinema, the psychotic's hallucinations are derived from the cultural repository of signs, which are reinvented and reconfigured into the personal. Just as the psychotic plays and invents through the languages that surround and contain him/her (speech, the body, the image, narrative, and so on), so does cinema reinvent its own textual languages through its films, through the vast historical and cultural orders, as well as through the actions of the spectator.

Within such reinventions and innovations the psychotic and the spectator reconstitutes him/herself through the different relationships of, experiencing the world, for one and watching a film, for the other which is also experiencing a type of world order.[49] And just as the spectator must more than merely understand the language of cinema, he/she must be a part of it – as in the case of psychosis: 'If the neurotic inhabits language, the psychotic is inhabited, possessed, by language' (Lacan 1993: 250). So the spectator can sometimes inhabit the language of cinema, and other times is possessed by that same language – a proposition that takes us back to Barthes' text of *jouissance*. For both of these positions will involve a type of excess – of subjectivity, of experience, of meaning, of pleasure, of reality.

This raises the further issue of the relationship between the psychotic and his/her hallucinations, and the cinematic spectator's relationship to those hallucinations produced by the film (in conjunction with the act of spectating as well). One of the seeming differences is that the film spectator knows that these hallucinations are not real; that they are after all only watching a film, and at some point soon this film will end, along with the hallucinations. The psychotic, on the other hand, is usually perceived as the mad person who does not know they are mad. In this sense, the hallucinations of the psychotic would seem to constitute their reality, whilst those of the cinema spectator are never really in contention for such a status (except for those moments when subjectivity is defined as that of the spectator). Lacan, however, argues an altogether different reading of the psychotic, and it is a reading that assists us in terms of the analysis of what it is to be a film spectator:

> in point of fact the madman doesn't believe in the reality of his hallucinations. . . . Reality is not the issue. The subject admits, by means of all the verbally expressed explanatory detours at his disposal, that these phenomena are of another order than the real. He is well aware that their reality is uncertain. He even admits their unreality up to a certain point. . . . Reality isn't an issue for him, certainty is.
>
> (Lacan 1993: 75)

Such a definition carries across to the film spectator, for when we watch a film there is never that sense of questioning reality as if it does not exist (we all know we are watching a film; that these films are of another order than reality), but the effect of the film on the spectator does bring an uncertainty of the status of the film as a type of reality. This is why, to return to an earlier point, there is no willing suspension of disbelief when we watch a film (or, to follow the historical origins of this phrase, read a novel for that matter), for like the psychotic what is at hand is the issue of certainty and not the question of reality.

There is another feature to the psychotic that relates to this idea of hallucination and cinema. At some point we must recognise that there are differences in a certainty that we hold that can be said to be 'true' and a delusional certainty that seems to have little basis in reality. Both carry with them the sense of conviction and may well be acted on, but there is a difference that will forever keep them distinct. The fear experienced in a horror film, or the sadness felt in a melodrama, is a delusional certainty (note that this fear or sadness has nothing to do with the status of the reality of the threat or tragedy – which is entirely hallucinatory), and even if we carry with us those same fears and anguish, it will always be delusional. So, for example, a midnight shortcut through a cemetery after watching a horror film continues the delusion of threat, confirms its certainty through a compelling sense of fear, but doesn't make it any more real. Similarly, the delusional certainty of invasion from aliens in the 1950s' science fiction films of Hollywood did not make such invasions (from outer space or Communism) any more real, but nor did it negate the sense of certainty. In a slightly different way this can also be seen as the historical reinterpretation that takes place in some films.

The cinematic version of historical events and places can become so strongly integrated into the social order that even if it is inaccurate there is a delusional certainty that overrides this (historical) reality. The rendering of a historical figure such as Billy the Kid (a noted sadistic killer) as heroic and handsome in Westerns means that reality has been replaced by this cinematic delusional certainty. The representation of white and black American service men as having a shared camaraderie in *Pearl Harbour* (Bay 2001) certainly bears little or no resemblance to the historical reality of the situation. Another, perhaps more complex example, is the representation of Hitler and Nazism as glorious and a cause for celebration in *Triumph of the Will* (Riefenstahl 1934). For those sorts of resonances to be possible means that the reality of the horror of Nazism must give way to a type of delusional certainty. Certainty is so powerful that it can override reality every time; like the psychotic, once we are certain it doesn't matter what the reality is.

Let us continue a little further with this idea of psychotic hallucination and its cinematic implications. Once we become spectators of a film we engage in a certain type of hallucination which, as we have noted above, demands certainty over reality. This is not to dismiss the issue of reality – the reality that exists outside of the film, the reality of the film's created world order, the reality of the spectator's relationship to the film, and so on. But the function of the cinematic hallucination is to enable such realities to co-exist, which is constitutive of being a spectator (even when these realities are in contradiction with one another). Once more, how cinema does this is comparable to the psychotic's relationships to reality and his/her phantasy world order. So when Lacan speaks of psychosis in the following way we can hear implications for cinema and its spectators:

What indicates a hallucination is this unusual sense the subject has at the border between the sense of reality and the sense of unreality, a sense of proximate birth, of novelty. . . . It is a created reality, one that manifests itself well and truly within reality as something new. Hallucination, as the invention of reality, here constitutes the support for what the subject is experiencing.

(Lacan 1993: 142)

This final sentence seems particularly striking in terms of cinema as a hallucination that comes to constitute a certain reality experienced by the spectator.

For both the psychotic and the cinema spectator the hallucination at once creates and sustains (that is, allows the experience of) a type of created reality and certainty. Such a comparison, it must be noted, can only be viable if one accepts the broader issue of the spectator's creative processes in the film. In other words, all those theories that argue for the spectator as creator can be seen to fit in with this reading of psychosis and spectators.[50] In this way, the spectator's own participation in the formation of the created world order of the film is also a participation in the formation of the hallucination. Such psychical (which must include the emotional as well as the spectator's own histories) investment and creativity is part of the pleasure of watching a film because it can be traced back to the formation and function of the ego. The model of ego and id are central to the formation of the spectator; just as the psychotic must re-read the world according to their position in it (and their interpretative phantasies), so must the cinematic world order be located within a frame of the spectator's ego-centricism and id-driven goals. Without these the image would lose its relevance, its meaning, and its sense of certainty.

The next difficulty for us here is to do with the insertion and escape from psychosis and the act of becoming spectator of a film. Here, we reach a point where the analysis of the spectator and psychosis seem to reach an impasse, and there is a very real temptation to fall back to the idea that neurosis might allow a better sense of the relationship between the spectator and the film. This is because psychoanalysis sees psychosis as particularly difficult in terms of the retreat from reality and the creation of a different, delusional, reality. There is certainly much to compel us to adopt this line of thinking that works with neurosis rather than psychosis. At times, there almost seems to be a sense that neurosis is something at the person's disposal, whereas psychosis is triggered and impossible to resist, and even escape. However, rather than refuse certain aspects of psychosis and spectatorship, there are a number of features that we can continue to tease out.

Lacan, via Freud, argues that the principle difference between neurosis and psychosis is that in the latter the delusional is so powerful that there is a complete abandonment of reality. Or, to be more precise (and it is a significant difference), what is at stake is the rejection of the Symbolic order, with its interpretation of the world and the subject. The issue for psychoanalysis is the difficulty by which the psychosis can be brought into a context of understanding (and, by implication, representation). This difference manifests itself at the level of the delusion: For Lacan delusions are 'legible', because of their relationship to the Symbolic. The delusion moves, as it were, into a different register. In these terms, cinema and its spectators must always remain at some level, like neurosis, in the register of the Symbolic. And yet, there is an aspect of the delusions of psychosis that can be seen as mirroring part of the spectating process.

When we watch a film there is a diverse range of possible narrating and viewing positions (that is, a heteroglossia, and multitude of different 'voices' or more accurately heterocular, a multitude of different gazes) of competing points of spectatorship. These are the demands of the film itself (which will include everything from narrative structures, the star system, the story, the techniques, the generic processes, and so forth), the cultural order that produced it (including sexualities, politics, race, economic forces, ideologies, and so forth and), our own cultural order, as well as our own personal histories. But one of the most significant spectating demands is the self for the self – that is, the insertion of the self (read ego) through a narcissistic drive. This will contain, among other things, the desire of the self for the self in all that is experienced, the sense-making processes of the narcissistic (such as the relevance to the self), the continual insertion of the ego into psychical activities. In short, it is impossible to escape the ego-centrism and narcissistic demands that are made, and these will make themselves felt whenever we become spectators. And it is at these points that the psychotic delusions, which are so driven by the narcissistic, re-emerge in the act of spectating.

Films gain their pleasures, and even their relevance, for the spectator when he/she participates in the delusion formation because it is at those moments that we come to possess a sense of the self in the text. To Freud's line in a letter to Fliess '*Sie leben also den Wahn wie sich selbst*' (a line Lacan enjoys so much he quotes it at least three times: '[Psychotics] love their delusion like they love themselves' (Lacan 1993: 157, 214 and 216) we can add that film spectators love their (cinematic) delusions because they see something of themselves (that is, construct themselves) in them. For the psychotic, this is the investment of the ego, via the id-drives, into the delusion; for the spectator, it is the same sense of ego and id-drives in the construction of the image. This is a construction that must take place in order for the subject to become a spectator. Without this cinema is impossible. This love (both narcissistic and for the image) is given more strength and power (including desire) through the spectator's own participation in the construction of the film, which includes this (psychotic) insertion of the self.

Clearly a process as complex as this must be something more than straightforward character identification. In fact, such identifications are almost antithetical to the processes currently under discussion because they do away with the delusional quality. Part of the process can be related to Lacan's idea of the *l'entre-je*, the between-I, which is the inmixing of subjects (Lacan 1993: 193). When the spectator participates in the delusional acts of watching a film part of the formation of pleasure is precisely this inmixing of subjectivities. In this case, it is the between-I of being a subject, a spectator, and the forces of the film itself. When we are film spectators we are something different to our everyday existence, and have a subjectivity that is a mixture of delusion, textuality and the self. And in this we witness part of the reason why being a film spectator is so pleasurable, for there is a great deal of power and seduction in the site of the between-I. In this position, the spectator finds him/herself in an extraordinary blend of realities and certainties that feeds delusions of immense force. The compulsion and seduction here is not that far removed from that of the psychotic's drive to escape.

A further feature of this between-I of the psychosis and the becoming spectator of the subject who watches a film is the state of flux between the subject positions (psychotic and sane, spectator and the subject in the everyday world). This is not simply a matter of sliding between states of subjectivity, but actually allowing the two to co-exist. For Lacan, psychosis involves a type of 'reasoning madness' (Lacan 1993: 217) because it has a type of logic that is essential to the madness itself. So we might see the watching of a film as a type of reasoned madness because it involves the capacity to hold the Symbolic (that of the everyday world) and the delusions (the created world of the film and the spectator's own creations) together at the same point in time. This is the way we can negotiate the seeming contradiction of reacting to the delusions of cinema as if they are real, all the while knowing that it is only a film.

The reasoned madness of watching a film – becoming a spectator – borrows from the processes of psychosis, it belongs to that same order of mental disturbances. This also goes some way in working through the issue of the self and identification. It was argued earlier that spectating is like psychosis in part because it is not the identification with a character, but an altogether more complex process involving delusion. As with psychoses, the act of becoming a spectator involves a continual negotiating of the self and Other. So the delusion becomes not a loss of a sense of the self (that is, what has been previously seen as character identification[51] and processes such as the willing suspension of disbelief), but a different relationship of the self to the Other. It would be difficult to overstate the significance of the Other within all of this, for here we find the formation of the spectator within the cinematic, and the articulation of the cinematic by the becoming spectator. Perhaps this is in need of some more, for at the level of the Other much is revealed about psychoses and, for us, cinema.

Let us take some of the fundamentals of Lacan's reading of the formation of subjectivity and its passage into psychosis through the interplay of the Other. From this, it will be possible to understand better the issue of psychosis and its function in cinema. So, to begin, let's compare some summary points. In Table 4.1 the left column offers some summary points of the Other (from Lacan), and those on the right position them in terms of cinema. After these columns appears Figure 4.2 which represents the spectator in terms of cinema and how this compares to Lacan's 'map' of the ego.

Table 4.1   Psychosis, the Other and Cinema

1 There are two others – the Other which contains all the otherness of the Symbolic order, as well as that of the unconscious. This is Otherness itself.	1 Cinema's Otherness exists within its position in the Symbolic. This is what locates the image outside of the subject.
2 And yet there are also two more others within this schema (see below) – so two others that are distinct from the Other. This is what Lacan terms the triplicity of the subject (Lacan 1993: 14).	2 The triplicity of the cinematic subject – which we have thus far articulated as the becoming spectator – is formed within, articulated as the becoming against, and through cinema's Otherness.
3 These two others are distinguishable in that one of them, the ego, is that which is employed by the subject to speak to the self. This is the 'normal' discourse of the self, or as Lacan puts it we speak to ourselves with this ego (see Lacan 1993: 14). It is because of this speaking to the self that a sense of the rational, socialised, 'non-mad' is created and sustained.	3 The ego employed to speak to the spectating subject is one that emerges from the field of cinema as a Symbolic process. The cultural training we receive in order to understand cinematic narration, composition of shots, cuts and edits, etc. are the rationalising ego of the subject who adopts the spectating site. This is the idea that films can make sense within themselves, and that watching them is a sense-driven act. Cinema declares itself as meaningful, and even if the meanings are unclear the spectator will pursue this ideal. This speaking ego is the one that demands the legitimation of the image for and by the spectator. In effect this is the speaking to the self through the cinematic image.
4 This 'dialogue' between the subject and his/her self is a normalising process, and is part of the function of the ego. The introduction of the Other is part of this process because, at one level at least, it helps the subject define his/her own sense	4 The spectating subject normalises the film experience through this function of the ego. We can read this dialectic of delusion as cinema, the other as spectator, and the Other as part of the reservoir of cinema (as well as cultural process, social

of self. We need Lacan at this moment: 'The distinction between the Other with a big O, that is the Other in so far as it's not known, and the other with a small o, that is, the other who is me, the source of all knowledge, is fundamental. It's in this gap . . . that the entire dialectic of delusion has to be situated' (Lacan 1993: 40).

5 The Other is also the unconscious, or perhaps more correctly, the unconscious is the Other. This is of course one of the great Lacanian themes, but in terms of psychosis it takes on a particular inflection. For Lacan it is the emergence of the speaking subject (the subject of the Symbolic in effect) that also marks the Other.[52]

6 Finally, Lacan continually returns to the idea that this relationship between the subject, the Other, and psychosis is in no small way organised through a dialectic. This is an unmistakably Hegelian dialectic, and one constructed around desire.

7 The relationship of the delusion and the Other is not just one of representation, but also of initialising: 'the delusion began the moment the initiative came from the Other' (Lacan 1993: 193).

history, the force of the unconscious to create desire in the image, and so on).

5 Cinematically speaking, the Other also functions in the formation of the spectator as psychotic. Without the cinematic Other there would be no psychosis because film itself would be undifferentiated from the events of the real world.

6 What he terms the line of imaginary relation we can reinscribe, without too much disturbance to the model, as the line of image relation.[53] And it is along this line that one of the primary dialectics is played out – between the subject and his/her sense of the self. In the psychotic subject this is formulated through hallucinations and total identification with the ego (for example, Lacan 1993: 14). This is also the line that we find the desire of and for the image, and what makes spectating so seductive.

7 The initiative of the cinematic delusion also relies on the operation of the Other, in this case the otherness of cinema itself.

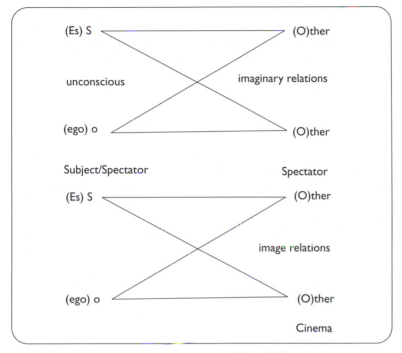

Figure 4.2   The ego schema and a cinematic variation
Source: Lacan 1993: 14. (See also Lacan 1988b: 232 for further details.)

There is tremendous complexity here, not the least because of the seemingly impossible attempt to constrain a slippery Lacanian formation – that of the Other/other – and match it against the almost unending productions and inventions of the cinematic apparatus. Our way forward is to keep in focus the primary objective here, which is the relativity of psychosis and spectating. And if such a thing is to be understood at all, it must take into account this idea that it is only through the Other that psychosis becomes recognisable. The function of the Other/other in the spectator is to allow image relations to take place. This is not identification, as has already been noted, but the dialectic of spectator to image through Otherness and desire. Interestingly, for Lacan what he terms the 'wall of language' (Lacan 1988b: 244) actually creates otherness for the subject, and in this sense the cinematic image (its wall of visual language) functions in the same way. Hence, not identification but alterity (that is, otherness) drives the spectator's relationship to the film. Furthermore, this offers a different sense to the operation of desire, for we do not desire through identification (or at least that would be a weak and surplus desire, a desire too easily constructed outside of ourselves), but we do desire through otherness. This is a theme that will be taken up in greater detail at a later point, for the moment we need to pursue the issue of delusions further.

One of the issues that this discussion leads us to is the status of delusion and its cinematic equivalent. Delusion is a key part of both neurosis and psychosis and the psychoanalytic interpretation of them; recall that it is the status of these delusions in terms of the subject and the real world that allows psychoanalysis to formulate differences between the two mental states. It is the relationship of the subject to his/her delusions that defines neurosis and psychosis, and, as has just been noted, their relationship to the world (Symbolic), self (Imaginary), and the Other. And all of this is negotiated through language, especially the visual when it comes to the psychotic, because they are the extreme version of the specular subject due to their particular relationship to the Imaginary. So the cinematic spectator may not be psychotic, and cinema does not actually bring on psychotic episodes, but in many ways the psychotic is the cinematic spectator *par excellence*.[54]

The status of delusions is deeply significant in psychosis, because they come to stand in for reality. Imagine an infinitely progressing line, one end reaches towards delusional psychosis, the other towards concrete reality (the actuality that events take place, that there are pebbles and trees, and so forth). We never stand at one end or the other, and we can also never really stand at that point in the middle, because no such point can exist. The line expands through history and cultural changes, so absolute concrete reality and absolute unimaginable delusions are never really there. There are certain things that cannot be contained on such a line. If towards one end we find the sand on a beach, and towards the other the memoirs of Schreber or the *enceeplate* of Rivière we are mapping out degrees of delusion and reality. These are degrees that will shift in time and across cultures (for example, the culturally constructed 'reality' of the earth as the centre of the universe becomes delusional after a time). But what of the star that shines in the sky at night? This may be as real as the sand, but no one has been there to show how it appears – we take its existence almost as an act of faith; it is not a delusion, but its sense of reality is almost as far removed from us as the words of the psychotic. And thus we also find the cinematic image – not real or delusion, but containing elements of both. For it to exist requires the specular subject who can hold both reality/realism and delusion at the same moment for the same image. The spectator must recognise the interplay of reality and delusion in order for the film to be able to exist, even if almost always we, as spectators, are unaware of this taking place. This is also part of the reason why the psychotic's delusion is more like what the cinematic spectator experiences than the usually theorised sense of phantasy. These delusions cannot be part of the satisfaction of desire that phantasy claims because their existence is for entirely different aims and objectives. The delusions of psychosis produce desire but are not the product of desire in the same way that phantasy is.[55]

This brings us to a phenomenon that, for want of a better phrase, we shall call the 'as if' sensation. Sometimes in films we are presented with a piece of information – a scene, a comment, a character's actions, and so on – that makes us mentally recoil from the 'reality' of the image/narrative, and we think 'as if that could happen!'. At these moments we find ourselves questioning the plausibility of what has just been presented to us. Yet these moments can, and often do, take place within a film that has the most delusional, the most implausible and impossible, of narratives and events. There may well have been many fantastical things that have already taken place within the narrative. The group of student film-makers in *The Blair Witch Project* (Myrick and Sánchez (II) 1999) is made up of young, affluent Americans with a solid knowledge of technology – so I ask myself 'as if none of them would have a mobile phone'! Yet why should this piece of improbability exist within a film that has so much improbability – is it that we can accept the existence of a witch in the woods more easily than affluent people without mobile phones? *Con Air* (West 1997) seems to recognise the 'as if' phenomenon and does not allow it to take place because for each of these moments there is another, more improbable than the last. At the very moment the spectator challenges an event the film simply exceeds that one with an even more excessive one. It displaces the 'as if' phenomena with excesses of these moments – a common strategy in the action genre.

Many of these 'as if' scenarios can be accounted for by slips in the narrative or formal constructions. That is, the film contains a type of inconsistency that the spectator cannot hold within the developments so far. Such inconsistencies can originate from disruptions to the textual expectations (such as narrative, genre, cinematic conventions of structure, and so forth) or from a disruption to the spectator's own sense of the film's development. This second order is part of the spectator's active construction of the film. At these levels (that is, textual inconsistencies or disturbances to the spectator's sense of things), these disruptions are usually seen as errors in the film. However, what these moments reveal, and some do this more readily than others, is the relationship between a type of psychotic delusion and the cinematic spectator. The 'as if' exposes the delusional qualities of the film – this is why we do not spend the entire time whilst watching a film questioning its plausibility, but can still have moments when this does take place. The mad, as Lacan tells us, exists in the Imaginary, and cinema is dominated by the Imaginary. The 'as if' moments are the disruption to the delusional madness of cinema's Imaginary.

At certain times these moments do not operate as textual errors, but rather indicate a refusal or resistance by the spectator to what is taking place on the screen. Such refusals, as with neurosis and psychosis, mark the disjunction between reality and hallucination, demonstrating that the two are different and yet entirely attached. When the spectator questions an aspect of the film that is not driven by some textual error what is taking place is a resistance to something within the film. If there is a refusal of the reality of the narrative then the 'as if' moment functions in the same way as a psychotic episode refuses a piece of reality and replaces it with a hallucination. In both circumstances, what is taking place is a defence through negation. So my questioning of a lack of mobile phones in *The Blair Witch Project* can also be seen to be a type of defence against an unconsciously motivated fear of rural isolation and the terror on the screen. Here, the 'as if' moment functions to allow pleasure within the experience of horror.

In summary then, there appear to be at least three aspects to the creation and function of the 'as if' phenomena: those derived from textual errors (the tractor wheels in the fields in *Gladiator* (Scott 2000), the lack of a shadow from the plane in the crop-dusting sequence in *North by Northwest* (Hitchcock 1959), and so on); those which indicate the delusional qualities of cinema itself; and those derived from a type of resistance by the spectator in order to find, or continue to sustain, pleasure in unpleasurable elements.

All three, although in particular the third type, are linked through variations on repression, which is quite in keeping with Lacan's sense of things when he states: 'repression is not the law of misunderstanding, it is what happens when things don't hang together at the level of the symbolic chain' (Lacan 1993: 84).[56] This issue of repression, refusal, and resistances will form the topic of the next chapter.

CHAPTER 5

The Hysterical Spectator against the Good

Our concern here is with a certain type of representational problem, that of the corporeality of hysteria, as well as the continuing interest in issues of spectatorship. When dealing with neurosis and psychosis we were aided or, perhaps more correctly, directed in our investigations through the consideration of versions of reality and how these came into play in the spectator's creation of, and attachment to, the cinematic signifier. However, with hysteria we encounter some altogether different issues and difficulties. We must resist readings and temptations such as those that would take up psychosomatic blurrings – of the spectator's body capitulating to a hysterical spasm of laughter, fear, and even the orgasmic (shadows of Charcot's exhibitionist scotomisation, of *scotome scintillant* and its *éblouissement de ténèbres*[57]) by the effects of the images and sounds of the film. Instead, our path will take us to a consideration of cinema's position as a cultural process, caught up in configurations of ethics. We do this to underline the relationship between madness and cinema as potentially disruptive forces of meaning through the resistance to the Law (which, as we shall observe shortly, is the larger order of moral and ethical demands).

This chapter begins with an examination of the relationship between the Good (the larger order of things related to defining a cultural sense of 'the good') and how it is manifested, that is the good (see note 58 below). We commence with this because one of our primary concerns here is how the hysteric challenges the order of things, and how this might be compared to the film spectator. Finally, we take up this approach because it allows us to investigate a certain type of relationship between psychoanalysis and philosophy. This will prepare some of the ground for the final chapter of the book. To consider this we shall begin with some ideas on the Good and the Beautiful. Thus formations of madness and the spectator are taken through the Good and the Beautiful towards a different appraisal of the cinematic sign.

On the Good

At various times, and in numerous ways, each of us is confronted with the issue of the good of what we do. This, of course, manifests itself in many different guises, with many different effects. Contained within such a confrontation are the issues of: is what we do any good? Does it produce the good? Is it a good thing to do? What are the goods it produces? Thus we encounter the range from production to value to ethics – and quite often, without a stumble in our pace, without pause and perhaps even without answer – we continue to do it. This is not a question of why we do what we do, but rather it is the issue of the relationship of what we do to the notion of the Good.[58]

So the issue at hand is what we do in the acts of watching and analysing a film (which also includes what the film itself does) in terms of the understanding and interpretation of the relationship of the good of what we do/films do. Paramount to such a discussion is the notion of a larger order of things, that is the Good. Included in this is the question of what is the relationship of what we do to any sense of the Good, and what is the position of madness in all this. And the answer to this question of our relationship, in madness, to the Good is a paradox, which can be dangerously summarised as: the goods (that is, the act of spectating, the analyses and interpretation of films, and films themselves) that we produce in and through madness must always run counter to the notion of the Sovereign Good (that is, a moral and ethical attachment to the Law) if they are to be any good (that is, to serve any purpose or be of any use to anyone). This forms part of the resistances essential to madness, that is, that which madness performs. There is always that tempting line of argument that would have us track down our discourses and statements, position the films, tracing them to the Sovereign Good because that is how we are supposed to think it, or at least that is how we might feel most comfortable. We do not simply want to be good at what we do, but we also want to have a sense that what we do is good. And therein lies the catch, for how can we ever know what should – let alone what does – constitute that good? The function of a certain force within cinema (that has been positioned here as a type of madness) is that it must always run counter to the notion of the Good; a definition of this cinema, then, becomes a site of resistance to the Sovereign Good. Once it becomes trapped in pursuing the line of the Law it loses both its critical power and identity; it comes to settle in a sort of complacency that pacifies and restrains. The force that drives the image with a sense of compulsion is lost in the moment of the Law.

We find a metaphor for this relationship between the Good and the entrapment of the complacent image in Lacan's mistrust, perhaps even hatred, of what he described as ego psychology. For him, much of this mistrust for, and resistance to, this version of psychoanalysis stems from the analytic quest to make people happy. This would seem to be an admirable aim, for it involves the easing of pain and the solving of disturbing problems. But Lacan's idea of psychoanalysis was far from such a model that contrived to get people to fit comfortably into, and without questioning (perhaps even unable to question), the social order. So much so that in 1954 he travelled to Lake Zurich to meet Jung hoping to find out something that would support his idea that Freudianism is inherently subversive – that is, runs counter to the notion of the Good. And from that private, almost clandestine, interview (which Jung himself had difficulty recalling) Lacan produced his famous statement the following year regarding Freud and Jung's trip to the USA. As they came to the shadow of the Statue of Liberty, Freud turned to Jung and said 'They don't realise we are bringing them the plague'. For Lacan, psychoanalysis should not feign the production of happiness, and so a version of complacency, but rather distress – 'the state in which man is in that relationship to himself which is his own death . . . and can expect help from no one' (Lacan 1992: 304). These are the great themes that Lacan discusses in his interpretation of desire through Kant and Sade. It is the problem of desire as a disruptive process that cannot be ignored, that will never go away, and the need to live cooperatively in a social environment. It is the question of how desire can be managed within the Law of the social order.[59] This idea that analysis should produce distress can be extended to include that broader field of analysis driven towards meaning and interpretation. This in turn can include the processes within critical theory and the analysis of films; and finally it can be seen as part of the function of cinema itself.

How reasonable is this? How much can we take Lacan's references to psychoanalysis and disturbance further than that particular theory and locate it within the field of cinema and analysis?
Within Lacan's own frame of reference this does not create much
of a problem. He himself compares it to something everyone does.
He positions this in terms of a question that everyone asks: 'The
question is, once it is over, once the return to the meaning of an
action has been accomplished, once the deep meaning has been
liberated . . . will everything work out all right by itself? Or, to be
precise, will there be nothing but goodness?' (Lacan 1992: 312).
The answer to this question is both an answer and another question. The answer – and it is the same one, unsurprisingly, given by
Lacan – is no; the question arising is how is it possible to even
speak of things like the liberation of deep meaning, or even a
return to meaning? And, finally, even if it were possible to have
such a thing, would we want the sort of goodness produced from
such analysis? This pacifying, homogenising seduction?

Hysterical flesh and the function of the beautiful

These are the broad themes of this chapter, and to consider a
particular inflection of them we will note a disjunction – the idea
of hysterical flesh, and the function of the beautiful. The title of
this section reflects the structure of the double bind – a structure
that attempts to organise, as much as is possible, a series of points
originating from this question of the good of what we do (as spectators, as film analysts, as producers of meaning). The idea that we
might conflate the paroxysmic visions of hysterical flesh, the
contradiction of the function of the beautiful, and the stumbling
point of the good of what we do, into one moment may seem
slightly perverse, if not impossible. And to hold it together with the
inherently unstable relationship of the double bind would seem to
add further disjunction. The perversion here works because the
double bind itself operates on the interchange of messages, each
dependant on the other, but each a different version.

Bateson, we recall, outlines a number of requirements for the
double bind, namely: a relationship between people; a primary
negative injunction along the lines of 'Do not do so and so, or I will
punish you' or 'If you do not do so and so, I will punish you'
(Bateson 1978: 178); a secondary injunction conflicting with the

first, operating at a more abstract level, and backed up by punishment; a tertiary injunction making escape from these two impossible. So anyone caught in the double bind situation cannot escape,
and cannot act without some form of suffering resulting.
Transgression and punishment are invested in the very materiality
of the double bind. Part of the consequence of this is that in the
double bind we are made to feel responsible for the events that
unfold, even if in the back of our minds is a sense of things being
unfair, and our position in it all feels foreign. And the back of the
mind that we have in mind here relates in no small way to the
unconscious and desire.

We can also note that within this idea of the double bind there
are the echoes of resistance. This operates in the very least at two
levels: there is the resistance given to us when we resist the
Sovereign Good – that is a sort of moral and ethical imperative, or
even a simple uneasiness of being resistant; the resistance towards
analysis itself. This second one is akin to what Derrida speaks of
when, within the context of psychoanalysis and philosophy, he
states: 'every resistance supposes a tension, above all, an internal
tension' (Derrida 1998: 26). This is a resistance which 'provokes
both the analytic and the dialectic to infinity, but in order to resist
them absolutely' Derrida 1998: 26). Derrida pushes this even
further when he goes on to argue that the double bind – with all
its attendant resistances – is the question of analysis itself (Derrida
1998: 36). Both these forms of resistances are tied up in the relationship of what is being called here hysterical flesh in and with the
analytic process. Hysterical flesh, then, is the site of resistance.

The operation of this is premised on the idea that the function
of the beautiful is the function of the hysteric. To understand this
we need to return to Lacan and consider how he contrasts the
beautiful with the Good. Lacan's play is with Good as the moral
good, and Good as the goods (in the sense of property) of economy. For him the Good is tied to a conflict between the good of the
Symbolic order (moral good and production) and the desires of
the unconscious. This is the idea we observed earlier in terms of
the Good and power. This is the enfolding and unrolling sets of
knots that Lacan sets up: the desires for the good of the self (ego)
are almost inevitably in contrast to the good of the Symbolic order;
and that these contrasts become linked to power and desire. The
surprising twist that Lacan applies to this is what he terms 'an
element of the field of the beyond-the-good principle' (Lacan

1992: 237), which we might expect to be excessive desire or *jouis-sance*, but which turns out to be the beautiful. But Lacan does not stray too far from the issue of desire here, and shortly after introducing this idea of the beautiful he states: 'The appearance of beauty intimidates and stops desire' (Lacan 1992: 238). So the function of the beautiful is at least twofold in these terms: it resists the power structures of the Good; it helps us cope with the potentially destructive moment of desire, and in particular *jouissance*. The beautiful comes to be positioned outside of the Symbolic order, and any manifestation of the beautiful is a weakened signifier, for it has been translated into a language system. It is culturally beautiful, but it is not *the beautiful*, and so does not have this function in terms of desire and *jouissance*.

These two components of hysterical flesh and the function of the beautiful can be utilised to work through the idea that we are constantly compelled to do things that run counter to what we want to do, that is, our desires, or what we are usually taught to see as the right thing to do. These are two quite distinct processes, but we can approach them from the same perspective. That is, how we operate in relation to the Good when the Good itself is brought into question, or our actions are questioned in relation to that Good. Further to this, how do texts operate within that exchange, and, in some cases, reveal the processes of this double bind? And how might these texts be seen as part of the participation in such processes, and even possibly an escape from them? The illustration here is how film provides a system of analysis for difference within the body when what is on display – the hysterical body – seems far removed from the idea of the Good body. This is the body formulated through the drives, as opposed to the filmic body; and the drives, Freud states, lie on 'the frontier between the mental and the physical' (Freud 1987: 108). From this metaphor comes the issue that what film, and the analysis of it, can perform is a sort of resistant good against the Sovereign Good. This will include film's performative function of the body to challenge the notion of the cultural and historically established Good. In terms of the analysis of film, this can also include things such as deconstruction's good against the Good of philosophy, feminism's good against the Good of patriarchy and phallocentrism, Lacan's good plague of psychoanalysis against the Good of ego psychology, Foucault's good of power/knowledge against the Good of institutionalised power, Lyotard's good

of multiple, little narratives against the Good of Grand
Narratives, and so on.

But, of course, the good of film and its analysis sometimes
resembles – and it is a necessary, often imperative resemblance –
that sort of radical evil that Kant positions in and against the
Sovereign Good. For Kant, we begin with this action towards radical evil, which is continually forced out by the Sovereign Good of
ethical behaviour – that is the superego. Radical evil works outside,
rather than against, the Sovereign Good, contrasted as it is to
Beauty as the symbol of the Good. To reinscribe Groucho Marx's
words when he is defending his client in court: 'This man looks
like an idiot and acts as an idiot, yet all of this should not deceive
you – he is an idiot'. So it is with Radical evil beyond Beauty: it may
look like evil, and may act like evil, but don't be fooled because it
is evil. But of an evil quite unlike that which ethics opposes to the
evil against the Good. To understand this some more we need to
turn to the radical of beyond the Good, and its relationship to the
function of a different sort of Beautiful. This we can do through
the metaphor of hysterical flesh.

The function of the beautiful can be seen as part of an odd
dialectic derived from power, the subject, and resistance. It is an
odd dialectic because the elements within it are contorted by the
processes of the dialectic, and it is not readily apparent how each
relates to the others. This oddity also allows us to preserve a certain
distance from the problems of dialecticism. The text's function
within all of this is a deeply complex one. At one level the text
performs the task of allowing manifestations of the beautiful to
take place. This is the goods (that is, the products) of beauty as
they are recognised in the Symbolic order – quite simply, what a
culture constructs as beautiful and the sorts of exchange currency
placed on it in terms of morality, value, and so on. There is also a
sense of a cultural appresentation of the beautiful (that is, a 'filling
out or completion by the cultural order) in this, which will include
how notions of the beautiful are constructed and sustained within
a textual field.[60]

The intimidation of desire by the beautiful

However, our concern here is with film's relationship to this idea
of the beyond-the-good and the intimidation of desire by the
beautiful. For, in this, we see a certain function of cinema, the

relationship of films to meaning, and another perspective on hysterical flesh. Such a distinction recalls Kant's ideas on the differences between the beautiful and the sublime. After noting that the beautiful and the sublime are similar in many ways, Kant spends time showing the differences, and one of the themes he returns to is the powerful, disruptive nature of the sublime. Thus he describes it as follows:

> if something arouses in us, merely in apprehension and without any reasoning on our part, a feeling of the sublime, then it may indeed appear, in its form, contrapurposive for our power of judgment, incommensurate with our power of exhibition, and as it were violent to our imagination, and yet we judge it all the more sublime for that.
>
> (Kant 1987: 246)[61]

These forces of the sublime are also part of what we describe here as the hysterical body in cinema. This is the body *sublimare* – lifted out of its ordinariness and held aloft. How such a body is positioned within cinema is part of the relationship between the beautiful and hysteria.

Here the relationships are constructed out of, and within, the various discourses of the filmic text. In other words, *the beautiful* is a textual discourse of cinema, *hysteria* is both the representation of the hysteric in cinema, as well as a certain property of the body within textuality, and *flesh* is the body, as a body, produced in and by the filmic text. The lines of connections represent the unending interconnection of texts (the transposition of narratives, images, actors, styles, and so on, across cinema) as well as the cinematic apparatus and textual orders that are used to construct ideals of the beautiful. These lines also represent certain types of relationships between the elements. The beautiful is positioned at the apex because in this construction of the diagram (see Figure 5.1) we are witnessing the production of a certain type of flesh that is bound up to hysteria, but it is important to realise that the actual location of the elements does not represent a hierarchy.

The first example of this is the fleshification of subjectivity. Or, how does a subject become body, a body become flesh? And the reverse of this – from flesh to body to subject. To fleshify the subject is to move him/her beyond even the body so that all meaning and interpretation is determined through flesh. This leads us to the function of the beautiful, not as a solution, as may first seem

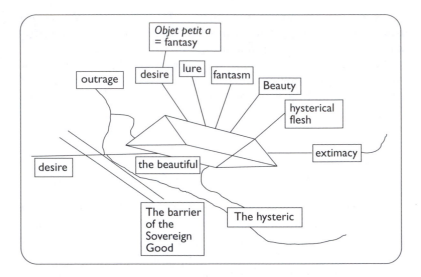

Figure 5.1   The prism of the Thing

to be the case, but as a concomitant action. And it is this action –
the action of disruption, resistance, aporia, fear, radical moments,
and so forth – that underpins our relation to the Good. Before this
is taken up we need to consider what we have labelled the prism of
the Thing/ *Das Ding*.

Figure 5.1 holds most of the themes of this chapter. The line of
desire should be imagined to look like a multi-stranded cable; so not
a single stranded, uniform desire, but rather polymorphic desires
which contain within themselves certain relational elements to the
two issues at hand: the compulsion towards the Sovereign Good, and
a (sometimes, indeed almost all of the time, conflicting) compulsion
to fulfil our desires. Contained within this, for example, will be
models of the beautiful that conform to a cultural order, and the
sublime, which can constitute a point of disturbance to that order.
Such a sense of conflictual compulsion within the desires is premised
on the idea that our drives run counter to the function of the Good.
This is the conflict between the Symbolic/Conscious/superego and
the various drives of our unconscious desires. Such a concept allows
Freud to speak of a tripartite morality, with the third version what he
terms civilised morality. This is dominated by the need to conform to
the morality of the cultural order, which almost invariably runs
counter to the desires of the unconscious.[62]

In such (Freudian) terms this is fairly straightforward. Nor is there anything especially unusual about the idea of a multi-stranded force of desire that contains within itself both the desire to adhere to this formation of the Good in the Symbolic, and the desire to oppose it because of how it represses desires and the process of desire itself. What stops desire from flowing on is what Lacan terms the barrier of desire on which the Good situates itself (see, for example, Lacan 1992: 218). To this he also adds the formation of the ego ideal – a site of resistance to the satisfaction of desire through the othering of desire itself (Lacan 1992: 234), and which has been positioned here as part of the barrier of the Good.

The other component, and perhaps the most significant, is power. Lacan argues that the barrier of the Good is actually formu-lated by and through power. As he puts it:

> The true nature of the good, its profound duplicity, has to do with the fact that it isn't purely and simply a natural good, the response to a need, but possible power, the power to satisfy. As a result, the whole relation of man to the real of goods is organized relative to the power of the other.
>
> (Lacan 1992: 234)

This is an essential point to grasp in Lacanian theory – desire's relation to the subject, to the morally and ethically defined good, to the Symbolic order, is one of power. And that which resists desire is a certain power, and not necessarily good. Furthermore, even if it is seen as good, there will still be a conflict with the aim of desire. In no small way this resonates in a critical fashion with Foucault's ideas on power/knowledge. For example: 'The exercise of power is not simply a relationship between partners, individuals or collective; it is a way in which certain actions modify others. Which is to say, of course, that something called Power . . . which is assumed to exist universally or in a concentrated or diffused form, does not exist. Power exists only when it is put into action' (Foucault 1983: 219). Part of the way power operates, indeed is formulated and inscribed, is through its relationship to the Good and the coercive management of desire, as well as the conflicts that arise from such desires. It would be tempting to leap in here and look for ways in which cinema, through madness, allows escape from this bind of the compulsions of desire and the need to comply with the Good. But let us hold this thought for a moment longer – there is still work to be done here.

This is the point, this complex genealogy of power and desire, this interplay between the Good and that which opposes it, at which Lacan would seem to have painted himself into a corner. His argument takes the following line: we cannot pursue our desires because they run counter to the Good (which here stands for the civilised morality); the Good, in turn, attempts to block our desires, transposing guilt onto them in an effort to make us turn from desire itself; we enter into a state of conflict because we have to give way to our desires – and this is the source of our furthering conflicts. In these terms, our desires become attached to the Kantian notion of Radical evil. But this would seem to suggest a sort of urging for the expression of all our desires no matter what the consequences. The subtle twist Lacan gives to all this (via, one suspects, a sort of Kantian-induced sense of the good will) is this notion of power. So, for example, Hitler's desires – the desires of fascism – are made to seem like the Good in a Nazi context, but they are really about a perverted power. The representation of such desire in something like *Triumph of the Will* illustrates a textual rendering of the Good and power. The film does not, in itself, bring into question the morality of Nazism and fascism because it functions within that context of the Good. This is not simply the process of ideology and glorification; it is the attempted absenting of the capacity to see this as anything but part of the Good.

Desire does not simply hit this barrier, but rather parts of it are drawn to it and others are forced towards it. Either way, desire eventually encounters this barrier and there are a number of actions and/or results, including repression, sublimation, conflict, guilt, and displacement. Desire cannot simply cross the barrier of the Good, but, argues Lacan, there is a way across into the 'field of the beyond-the-good principle' (Lacan 1992: 237) – and, somewhat surprisingly, it is the beautiful. In typically Lacanian fashion, he does not simply argue that the beautiful allows desire to continue. Rather, that it is a special sort of relationship between desire and the beautiful that allows the barrier of the good to be crossed: 'This relationship is strange and ambiguous. On the one hand, it seems that the horizon of desire may be eliminated from the register of the beautiful. Yet, on the other hand, it has been no less apparent . . . that the beautiful has the effect, I would say, of suspending, lowering, disarming desire. The appearance of beauty intimidates and stops desire' (Lacan 1992: 238). How are we to make sense of such a relationship? Desire and the beautiful are joined as a site of resistance, and a force of crossing, to the barrier of the Good, and yet beauty also eliminates desire from its own form, and even has the effect of stopping it. There would seem to be a fundamental conflict within all this. However, Lacan argues that there are times when the two can be combined in what he describes as outrage. This idea of the joining leads Lacan to the following: 'Moreover, it seems that it is in the nature of the beautiful to remain, as they say, insensitive to outrage, and that is by no means one of the least significant elements of its structure' (Lacan 1992: 238). This insensitivity of the beautiful allows it to exist beyond the barrier of the Good. It is also what reunifies it with the sublime (recalling that, for Kant, they share a great deal).

This is a great term here, this *outrage*. We emerge from a breaking through of the barrier of the Good, into the field-of-the-beyond-the-Good through a combination of desire and the beautiful – a construct of double binds – produced through, and producing, outrage. This outrage is the shout from the Symbolic order of the Good, and the problematics of the double bind of a beauty that does not exclude desire. It is the force of the sublime as it creates the turmoil of the mind in the apprehension of the image.

What does this mysterious force encounter? Many things, but three will be nominated here: an offshoot of outrage which escapes repression but is made manifest as a type of antisocial process, or that which resists the pacifying textual order (film and its spectators outside of the pleasurable and as *jouissance*); the spectator as hysteric in the field of the sublime; and the construction and operation of the beautiful. What happens within each of these processes is impossible to definitively describe for there is never a universal pattern to all this, and further splintering must always take place. Part of the effect for all of them must be to encounter *Das Ding*, which is represented here as a prism which will fragment these elements further, much as white light is split into a multiple of colours when it passes through a prism. *Das Ding* is Lacan's term (via Freud) to denote the strange, the unknowable, the unrepresentable, the foreign, the outsideness and Otherness. He introduces it to negotiate an interpretation of the opposition of the reality principle and pleasure principle. There is subtlety in Lacan's progression here; *das Ding* holds the true secret, as Lacan puts it (Lacan 1992: 46). This is the secret of how Need (as distinct from needs) ends up driving us from reality, so that the reality principle in fact 'isolates the subject from reality' (Lacan 1992: 46). *Das Ding* is the 'absolute Other of the subject' (Lacan 1992: 52) that, according to Lacan, we continue to search for through our desires, swept along through the manifestations of the pleasure principle. Opposed to this is the Good of the reality principle. So in effect *das Ding* is that which we know nothing of – the eternally strange – and yet at the same time it is the absolutely familiar. We are tempted, no doubt, to look for aspects of the *unheimlich* here – and there certainly are connections. Freud's idea of the uncanny as that which contains the familiar and the strange at the same moment does fit nicely here. However, perhaps of more relevance here is Lacan's idea of extimacy.[64]

Extimacy is Lacan's term to deal with the issue of the Real in the Symbolic; it is that which is more intimate than the most knowable, intimate detail, yet to confront it is to see a fearsome thing. The Lacanian Real is extimacy, being as it is more real than reality, so much a part of our psychical processes, and yet so foreign to our conscious mind. The extimacy of our desires resides in a Radical evil for they define our subjectivity, and yet resist any Symbolic compromise.

From this prism effect a number of splits have been nominated, but of course they are by no means complete. Nor should they be seen as somehow fundamental to this process, nor universals in what is ultimately an unrepeatable process. They do signify a number of possibilities, and to illustrate a couple of them further the next part of this discussion will trace the line of hysterical flesh as it emerges out of the extimacy of this prism to produce a corporeal *Thing* (that is, a cinematised version of the body as *das Ding*) which is no less than the body in film. This means that all bodies in film can be read as a type of hysterical flesh – this is part of what cinema does to the body. In other words, once the body becomes a filmed one it always has some aspect of hysterical flesh attached to it.

All of the examples here are based on the idea that there is a certain relationship between the body, desire, and the beautiful. To say that such a relationship exists is stating the obvious, particularly within the cinematic context; but this is what makes things all the more interesting. We accept the relationships of desire, beauty, and bodies because that is how these three are constructed within film. Even when they are opposed to that (a body less beautiful, undesirable; a beauty outside of corporeality), what renders the quality of opposition is precisely the measure against this paradigm. The intervention of extimacy is when one of the elements overcomes the others so that the familiar is made strange. It is, as noted earlier, the question of the Real in the Symbolic, so that the qualities of the Symbolic-defined body (such as the culturally beautiful or the gender-constructed body) must be measured against a different Real. This is the beautiful body as the Thing; our desire for it as extimacy.

What this suggests is that, as with the Good, we need to at least attempt to differentiate between senses of the beautiful. Or if such a typology seems impossible, then at least acknowledge such differences. Part of the function of the beautiful as it emerges out of the prism of the Thing is to allow the subject his/her desire – our heart's desire no less. It does this because the beautiful of extimacy is attached to desire, it does not deny desire's existence, and allows us the right to desire. Of course the difficulty here, and it must be a future project, is what to do with the evil of certain desires, or how do we deal with those desires that run directly counter to the notion of the Good.

Hysterical flesh and the substance of fantasy

At one level this extimate beauty, which has as its function nothing to do with an ideal beauty, allows us to desire and produces various objects of desire which become the substance of fantasy (such as Lacan's *objet petit a*). Cinematised bodies are such objects, functioning as they do in a relationship between the split subject and alienation and aphanisis.[64] This is the split subject of the spectator, as well as the various splits within the discourse of the image, including the subject made flesh through a filmed body. These are the terms in which the bodies are versions of the sublime hysterical flesh. The whole set of processes, including the challenge to meaning through the body, we shall designate as hysterical flesh. *Hysteria* because this is a term that has always been connected with the conflation of the mental and corporeal; *flesh* to denote a change in the reading of the body because of this hysterical manifestation and identification.

Our definition of hysterical flesh, then, is: The representation of the body when it exceeds, transgresses, challenges, and resists its moral, ethical, social status and in doing so comes to problematise meaning systems and interpretations. It is the subject made flesh by a collapse in the systems of signification, because meaning itself becomes entrapped within the physical. It is the resistance of certain power structures (the Symbolic order with its moral codes) by certain power structures (unconscious desires, the antisocial body, and so forth) formulated in the function of the beautiful and its attachment to desire, played out though the body. It is the (Kantian) sublime constructed out of a body that resists ease and comfort, that will shake our sense of what the body is. Hysterical flesh is a challenge to meaning initially through the body (as what that signifies is undone) and then to other forms of meaning and interpretation, such as the cultural hermeneutics. It is the negotiation of meaning through the body that challenges the epistemes through the conversions of flesh. It is also something that is played out within four large orders: the realm of the impossible signifier; the powers of institutions; the formation of gender; the formations of subjectivities. Finally, it is part of the sublime in its capacity to create apprehension in the spectator; that is *apprehendere* – to seize. In this, the spectator is seized, is held, and is filled with tremulous understanding.

Hysterical flesh is formulated within the realm of impossible signifiers because its very existence is a challenge to how systems of representation work. Here we have a corporeal construction that signifies not the body, but the mind. The filmed body is no longer the body, but something belonging to the impossible signifier. For the primary motivation of meaning (that is, what the spectator sees as a sort of interpretative grounding) of hysterical flesh is carried by the body, but traced back to the Thing. Its representation as a signifier is impossible because of this conflict and contradiction. The corporeality of the body functions as the beautiful as well as beauty, because it comes to stand for a series of cultural and personal variations on the morally and ethically good. In these terms, it operates in what Lacan calls the fantasm, which is 'a beauty that mustn't be touched' (Lacan 1992: 239), and it is only once corporeality loses this status (to become beautiful and desiring, rather than the beautiful) that it enters the social domain. The power of institutions is derived from this opposition, for it is the resistance of the body to those systems that attempt to mark it, place it, and interpret it. Historically, this helps to explain the connection of hysteria to women's bodies. It is the phallocentric institutions of the body (including sexualising/eroticising the body, dressing it, gazing at it; the medical positioning of the male and female bodies, the punishment and disciplining of the body, through the body) which offer interpretations of how the body should be and act which hysterical flesh resists. This relates to the gendering of the body, which very much marks the corporeal within a social construction. This is not the physical differences of the body, but the cultural processes (including, of course, cinema) of engendering. Hysterical flesh resists the normalising – that is, in effect, the ideal beauty of the Good – of such specific gender categories and processes. Finally, this relates to the construction of subjectivities, for hysterical flesh brings into question the role and function of the processes of subjectification by the Symbolic order. Such subject positions cannot be safely handled by that order, operating in a space that is neither within the social construction of subjectivity, and yet is not totally excluded from it.

This in-between status provides us with the second key aspect to the filmed body, but to understand this we shall take a less obvious example to begin with. Derrida recounts how, after a preliminary arrangement for him to coordinate an exhibition at the Louvre, he developed a viral infection:

> With the exhibition already envisaged, I have to cancel a first meeting at the Department of Drawings. . . It is July 5th, and I have been suffering for thirteen days from facial paralysis caused by a virus, from what is called a figore (disfiguration, the facial nerve inflamed, the left side of the face stiffened, the left eye transfixed and horrible to behold in a mirror – a real sight for sore eyes – the eyelid no longer closing normally: a loss of the wink or blink, therefore, this moment of blindness that ensures sight its breath). On July 5th this trivial ailment has just begun to heal. It is finally getting better after two weeks of terror – the unforgettable itself – two weeks of vigilant medical attention. . . And so on July 11th I am healed (a feeling of conversion or resurrection, the eyelid blinking once again, my face still haunted by a ghost of disfiguration). We have our first meeting at the Louvre. That same evening while driving home, the theme of the exhibition hits me. All of a sudden, in an instant. I scribble at the wheel a provisional title for my own use, to organise my notes: *L'ouvre ou ne pas voir* (The Open Where Not to See).
>
> (Derrida 1993: 32–3)[65]

The play Derrida sets up between the Louvre – one of the most amazing and stimulating art collections ever known – and the

open reads so well in his ecstatic re-vision in the car. The open –
like the eye – where not to see; the Louvre – the great building of
art – where not to see. In a way Derrida's revelation in the car is
not dissimilar to Lester Burnham's moment when he first sets eyes
on Angela in *American Beauty*. They both confront a great moment
of fear through the beautiful. Their flesh is rendered hysterical –
recall how Lester states his aim for running is just to look good
naked; Derrida offers such a sense of need when his face returns
to normal – it would seem that looking good naked is just as important to philosophers as it is to American salesmen. What is also
being confronted in these examples – Derrida's paralysis, Lester's
beautiful object of desire in a bed of roses – is the double bind
(with its resistances and analysis). For as Derrida argues:

> a double bind cannot be assumed; one can only endure it in passion. . .
> if a double bind is never one and general but is the infinitely divisible
> dissemination of knots, of thousands and thousands of knots of
> passion, this is because without it, without this double bind and with-
> out the ordeal of aporia that it determines, there would only be
> programs. . . and no decision would ever take place.
>
> (Derrida 1998: 36, 37)

This is the order of passion and blindness that drives Lester to live
differently.

Lester's hysterical flesh stands in for the emptiness of his life –
this is the Thing that splits ordinary life that incorporates ordinary
evil, from the sort of Radical evil that everyone associates with his
actions (which will include the discomfort people have with his
desires for Angela). This is the ordeal of the aporia that allows him
to take those life-changing decisions. The function of the beautiful
– a sort of American beauty made ironic – allows the crossing of
the barrier of the Good; just as it is Lester's desire that separates
him from the others in that suburban life. Derrida's transfixed eye
and paralysed left side of his face – the unforgettable terror –
allows him to formulate a type of beauty that becomes the exhibition at the Louvre. As with all hysterical flesh, the beautiful seems
to emerge out of them, but in fact it is the function of the beautiful (in this sense of the sublime) to allow desire to engage in the
Thing beyond the Good. In this sense it is both Lester's and
Angela's bodies that become sublime versions of hysterical flesh –
Lester's through a transformation of subjectivity, Angela's through

a radical version of the self to the self. These two bodies become hysterical through perversions of temporal orders – Lester's body travels back in time to roads not taken in youth, Angela's body travels forward in time to appear as more sexually advanced than it actually is. Similarly, Lester's body becomes the sublime version of resistance for other people. It is the gay body for Colonel Fitts, the transgressive adult body for Ricky.

It is now time to turn to another set of examples in order to map out further the relationship between the filmic body and these themes of the Good, hysteria, and flesh. Our first example, *Psycho*, will be one where the relationship between the hysterical body and the body as flesh is positioned as oppositional. Part of the rationale for commencing with this film is that it is so well known, so well discussed, that its imagery and sounds have become synecdochic for certain cinematic versions of fear and terror. This almost over familiar sense of the film makes it an interesting example to tease out further issues of extimacy and the construction of the Thing.

At one level, the most straightforward part of this positioning of extimacy is with Norman, and it is the site of Woman that presents the slippage. His body is hysterical flesh as it is contorted across genders, as it becomes the site in which conversion hysteria (perhaps one of the most direct manifestations of hysteria through the body) is played out (through the voice, clothing, and sexuality), and as the power struggle between a whole range of 'systems' of symptoms and cultural models of madness. These include: mother/son, male/female, freedom/prison, violence/passivity, rational/madness, human/animal, moral/immoral. We also witness examples of anxiety hysteria, particularly in the shot compositions and actions that associate him with the carcasses of birds. The inability of flight (from the past and in particular his mother), the morbid images, the 'bird's-eye' view (which becomes translated into the spying of Marion in the shower) are all parts of the projection of Norman's psychopathologies onto external objects.

It is also the body which forces the hysterical acts, as Norman is torn between sexual desire and the repressive morality of the Mother. And it is this same construction of the hysterical body of sexuality that allows Norman to position Marion's body as flesh. This body, sexualised as part of the Symbolic order of beauty, is made flesh at least twice in the film. The first is in the opening scenes where Marion and her lover are seen in bed in bright daylight. This is the flesh of sexual transgression. The second time is the shower scene, where her subjectivity is rendered as flesh through desire (the scopophilia of the camera) and then subjected to Norman's hysterical flesh. Significantly, the link between these two is through the cinematic devices rather than any direct narrative binding. In other words, the positioning of Marion as flesh is not dependent on Norman's gaze, because it has already taken place before he enters the narrative. Because we find out later that this attack was performed by Norman, and not Mother (as is first implied), this quality of hysterical flesh is a conflation of Norman and Mother, as well as a conversion of Norman's body onto Mother, and vice versa.

Psycho produces different types of hysterical flesh, including the horror of embalmed flesh, the mutilation of the *corps propre* (in particular the feminine in Mother and Marion), as well as the spectator's own flesh. The shower scene, as well as other killings such as that of Arbogast, operate very much as techniques of horror to make our, the spectator's, skin crawl. But beyond these versions of hysterical flesh as terror, it is important to recognise that the scenes of Marion as sexual agent, as thief, as transgressor, are also of this order of the body. Hysterical flesh is not simply the repulsive, for it can also be the most extraordinarily compelling and visually exquisite.

The positioning of Mother as the beautiful may seem strange, for this figure (as a remembered character, as Norman's perverse reanimation of her, and the semi-embalmed corpse sitting in the chair at the end of the film) is always abject. However, what is important to remember is that the construction of Mother is derived from a number of different sources. At one level, Mother is a hysterical version of motherhood, which is normally a primary source of the beautiful, both as the Good and goods (the cultural propriety of motherhood). This is constantly asserted through the reference to her as Mother, and only occasionally as Mrs Bates. This is also the beautiful as it is derived from a warping process of power, which in turn stems from the psychopathologies of hysteria and subjects made flesh. In other words, we need to read this model 'up' from the positioning of hysteria and flesh, for this is where Mother is constructed. Marion's body is beauty located within desire, Mother is the beautiful as it intimidates desire and produces hysteria.

This is construction that can be seen almost as a type as it is found in many different guises. The beautiful Mother of Claire

Bartel in *The Hand That Rocks the Cradle* (Hanson 1992), for example, is set against the sublime Mother of Peyton. As with Mrs Bates, Peyton loves, and is loved, beyond the Good. Her acts of mothering are perversions of love, but are always motivated by a sense of the Good. Just as Norman, as Mother, acts out of extreme ethical adherence to a version of motherhood (to protect the child), so Peyton provides a version of the Mother that holds at its centre the preservation of the family. The Good of the Mother is derived from this sense of the family and versions of things such as sacrifice, trust, and nurturing. This is how the figure of the other mother (Norman as his mother, Peyton as the more-than-the-mother for the children – she breastfeeds the baby, protects the daughter from bullies) becomes a twisted version of the Good. These foregrounded attributes invest these figures with a sense of the Good played out in the cinematic versions. Note, for example, the absolute trust placed in the strangers (particularly the woman, Mrs. Drayton, who is given the son) in *The Man Who Knew Too Much* (Hitchcock 1956) and yet the lack of trust in the police or close friends.

The second example may help clarify this relationship. This time we will focus on the relationship between the beautiful positioned as the opposite of flesh in *High Noon*. The hysterical can be located in a number of different ways, but since our primary interest here is the manifesting of the mental through the body (especially in terms of power) one of the key examples of this is Will Kane. It is his body that becomes the site where all issues of morality and ethics are played out, including the social (the inability and inaction of the townspeople), the sexual (his past sexual relationships as well as his current and future ones), and the personal. These are no more clearly demonstrated than in the countdown to noon scene, prefaced by his writing of a will, and closed by the sound of the train's arrival. In this sequence (and the surrounding ones), there are a number of shots which emphasise the body as vulnerable flesh (the shave, the cuts on his face from the fight, the flexing of the sore hand), even the shot of the empty chair (an absent reminder of Frank Miller) serves to position the body as the key signifier in the playing out of a cultural order of ethics. The lacuna of Miller's flesh drives the narrative as well as all the emotions.

Amy Kane's (as well as Grace Kelly as that character) corporeality functions as the beautiful as well as beauty, because it comes to stand for a series of cultural and personal variations on the morally and ethically good. In these terms, it operates on the level of the Lacanian fantasm, which is 'a beauty that mustn't be touched', and it is only once she loses this status (to become beautiful and desiring, rather than the beautiful) that she enters the social domain of Helen Ramirez.[66] The intimidation of desire here is quite the opposite of that found in *Psycho's* Mother, for it is a sense of purity that frames this version of the beautiful.

To understand how this functions in the character of Amy Kane we can return to Lacan's attempts to work out in more detail the relationship between the beautiful and desire. At first, he suggests that there is an element of this relationship that causes desire to be excluded from the 'register of the beautiful' (Lacan 1992: 238). However, he then argues that there are times when the two can be combined in what we have noted earlier as mysterious, for it is the quality of remaining insensitive to outrage. This is precisely what we find in the joining of desire and the beautiful in both Grace Kelly, the actor who comes to culturally signify this, and the character within the film. It is the multiplicity of outrages that propels much of the narrative of *High Noon*, including the antithetical range of Miller's desire for revenge and the outrage symbolised in the final shots of the badge being thrown into the soil by Kane. However, Amy Kane travels a complex path in terms of this attribute, and this is how she moves between the beautiful, with its insensitivity to all the outrage, and desire when she has to participate in it. Positioned in this way, her choice becomes one of the beautiful contained within her pacifist politics, and desire contained within her romantic love of Kane. Helen Ramirez is more clearly delineated as flesh compared to Amy Kane's status of the beautiful (thus evoking a subtext of racial stereotypes). This is true not only of her more overt sexuality, but also due to the linking of her past with both Will Kane and Frank Miller. Here, desire overcomes (cultural) beauty.

Each of these three characters demonstrate, at different times, qualities of hysterical flesh. As noted above, the foregrounded body of Will Kane gives away his fears and anxieties; Amy Kane becomes hysterical flesh when she has to decide whether to return to town (and so become a participant in violence) or not; Helen Ramirez's gaze of knowledge (for it is her gaze that demands most of all three characters), particularly in the final shot composition before choices are made and noon approaches, turns her own body into hysterical flesh, and makes incisions in the others. Compare this to Kane's gaze as he confronts the townspeople and their lack of support. His gaze is harsh and commanding, and yet he is the one who walks away with head bowed. But of the three, it is Amy Kane that is the least rendered as flesh, in part because she is foregrounded as the spiritual for much of the film.

The third example is one where the beautiful is transformed into flesh via a type of hysterical force and drive. This example is taken from *Die Hard* (McTiernan, 1988) because in this film we find a structuring of the male body as the beautiful as it accumulates wounds. Much like the paintings of the martyrdom of saints (St. Sebastian is a particularly good example), the body of John McClain clearly and constantly bears the wounds gained from the events. They operate as signatures of events on flesh, each one carefully retained until the end of the film. (Compare this to many similar films where the body seems to heal miraculously and always returns to a 'cleansed' form – the *corps propre*). Such is this process of accumulation that in the final sequences where McClain confronts the criminals his body is almost entirely bloodied, and his wife struggles to recognise him. McClain's body does not, of course, start like this. In fact, it is the contrast of the Bruce Willis body as powerful, perfectly masculine (slowly exposed for the spectator in a violent striptease), and complete to the contused and lacerated body that produces a form of hysterical flesh. We also see this in, for example, the body of Tom Cruise in the *Mission: Impossible* films. Muscles are made hysterical versions of themselves in the suspended body sequences (the lowering into the room on cables in the first film, the Christ-like suspension on the cliff in the second). These are the sublime muscles, they are the muscles of the Thing.

With these sorts of examples we find much less the literal manifestation of hysteria (such as the conversion hysteria in *Psycho*) and more a type of hysterical flesh derived from social and personal sacrifice. In these terms, the body is transformed from a sense of the beautiful into flesh via a hysterical process that involves the psyche of a cultural order. It is the *mythos* of the sacrifice of the masculine that produces this flesh. Significantly, this version of the sacrifice is linked to the figure of the *pharmakos* – the scapegoat who is both the remedy for, and the cause of, suffering. Derrida proposes that the character of the *pharmakos* involves both 'the *evil* and the *outside*, the expulsion of the evil, its exclusion out of the body (and out) of the city' (Derrida 1981: 130). Furthermore, the *pharmakos* occupies an unusual site, neither apart of or a part from the cultural order: 'The ceremony of the *pharmakos* is thus played out on the boundary line between inside and outside, which has as its function ceaselessly to trace and retrace' (Derrida 1981: 133). What is significant for the concerns here is that it is this liminal quality, the neither included nor excluded and the need to continually retrace, which produces hysterical flesh. The body of McClain is rarely (if ever) positioned within the social order (he exists in abandoned floors of incomplete buildings and airport tunnels, in elevator shafts, basements and rooftops); it is also, through its violent wounds, that the body is made more and less than human. The abjection of the blood is 'saved' by the sense of sacrifice.

Although films such as *Die Hard* and *Mission:Impossible* function very much outside of the tragic form, constantly observing the function of heroic success against all adversity, there is a passage in Lacan that can be used to open up another facet of hysterical flesh in filmic texts. Speaking of *Antigone* (and a long philosophical tradition of commentary on that text) Lacan arrives at a point regarding the 'effect of beauty on desire' (Lacan 1992: 248), which is this element of tragedy. This effect is derived from tragedy's drive of death in life, of 'the meaning of the situation or fate of a life that is about to turn into certain death, a death lived by anticipation, a death that crosses over into the sphere of life, a life that moves into the realm of death' (Lacan 1992: 248). This describes the torments of McClain, with the exception that although death seems certain at every turn, it is always evaded. Nonetheless, these are lives lived in anticipation, and it is the constant reminders of death that makes the flesh hysterical, and the subjectivity of the character most precarious.

One of the fundamental points that draws all these examples of hysterical flesh together is that the site at which meaning is situated is the body. Even though in each case the emphasis is on a meaning situated elsewhere (the mad mind of Norman, the social, religious and personal sacrifice of Amy Kane, the *pharmakos* of McClain), its manifestations and interpretations are tracked to the body made flesh. Meaning thus becomes problematised because there is a need to produce interpretation out of a system convoluted with disguise, repression and conversion. Hysterical flesh demands interpretation – it is specular and forceful, it is the cinematic apprehensive – but where such meanings are generated, and how they are sustained is equally part of the process.

The spectator's hysterical body

Now we must turn to an altogether different aspect of hysteria as it becomes a version of the sublime in the body, which can have the consequence of the sublime body of cinema. This, we recall, is the position of the spectator as he/she engages in the corporeality of the film; it is the merging of volatility and the attempts to understand in the apprehension of the beautiful as it interrupts the Good. Throughout our discussions we have been concerned with a number of issues related to madness and cinema, including the questions such as: what is it to be a spectator of a film? What happens to us when we become the subject who spectates? And, finally, in this particular discussion, what is the relationship of this spectator to the hysterical flesh of cinema? These are, in fact, the questions that the hysteric asks. Lacan's point about Dora, as she has come to almost typify the positioin of the hysteric, is that there is a continual questioning of what it is to be a woman. The hysteric asks this because they are caught in the impossibility of their self as it negotiates the world. The hysteric's question, then, is related to how we all position ourselves in, and are positioned by, the forces of our culture. Thus the cinema spectator, experiencing a body made flesh and sublime, is allowed the question that the hysteric has. *Allowed* because in order to be articulated (that is, taken up and engaged in) the spectator must first overcome the Good. Once more, this has a parallel in hysteria. The hysteric's question emerges through the two key aspects of lack and desire. For them, it is an interplay derived from a sexual source – their sexuality is based on lack, their desires are fundamentally thwarted. It is through this curious relationship that their whole interaction with the world is founded.

The spectator's question of what it is to be a spectator is a doubling process. There is the complex engagement of becoming a spectator, and there is the encounter with the cinematised body, which will include its evocation of itself as the sublime. Both of these processes lead back to the position of hysteria because both of them require, at some point, the questioning of the relationship to the signifier. These two are enfolded because one initiates the other. Once more we must note that all cinema holds this phenomenon *in potentia,* just as all spectators are capable of constructing this (but may not), and yet not all cinematic signs will perform this role. Perhaps this is necessary, for cinema would become the impossible repository of spectatorship if this level of disruption and self-reflexive questioning took place all of the time. The fact that such questioning rarely takes place is part of the requirement of textuality; the fact that it is always possible is an attribute of that same textuality.

So what is it to be faced with such a hysterical moment of the sublime beauty of the cinematic signifier? What it is to ask the question of what is it to be the subject who asks 'what is it to be a spectator'? This, as we have seen elsewhere, cannot rest simply in the representation of the sublime, or the beautiful for that matter – and yet these are key elements in the process. There cannot be a universal image, or passage of narrative, that can compel all who witness it to go beyond the pleasurable into *jouissance.* It cannot even be said to lie within a certain type of cinematic sign or form. Ultimately, it is the experience of being a spectator that actually enables the hysteric's question to be asked. This is the realisation of a lack, the sensation of a desire, and the pursuit of the cinematic sign. And within all this is a certain epistimophilia, for the spectator, in asking the hysteric's question, also asks about meaning and knowledge. This is why madness – the otherness of such things – can be seen as an essential part of the cinematic apparatus.

Knowledge is something we shall take up in more depth in the following chapter, but let us stay with this for the moment. Lacan's idea that the hysteric, through his/her symptoms, is asking the question about being and their place in the world. In doing so they also ask the questions about meaning. Our task here is to compare what the hysteric does in such an inquiry to what cinema requires of the spectator. This returns us to an earlier point regarding neurosis, psychosis and identification. For, in the hysteric's question, we encounter an underlying motif of crisis through identification – and this is tied to knowledge.

Let us compare a passage from Lacan about the hysteric to the spectator:

> The domain of knowledge is fundamentally inserted into the primitive paranoid dialectic of identification with the counterpart. The initial opening of identification with the other, that is, with an object, starts from here. An object is isolated, neutralized, and as such particularly

eroticised. This is what makes an infinitely greater number of objects enter the field of human desire than enter animal experience. In this interweaving of the Imaginary and the Symbolic lies the source of the essential function that the ego plays in the structuring of neurosis.

(Lacan 1993: 177–78) (translation modified)

Working from the end backwards, as it were, this final sentence recalls the position of cinema (the interweaving of the Imaginary and Symbolic) as it is formed by the spectator. The ego's structuring of neurosis is part of the negotiation of the different versions of reality encountered in the constitutional process of watching a film. The cinematic object, as we have noted elsewhere, is erotised in this process – it is what makes the watching of a film both possible and meaningful. It is also where cinematic desire, conflated with that of the spectator, is to be found. It is the cinematic apparatus that performs the task of isolating such objects, with neutralisation here being read as the construction of such objects outside of the real world and within a created world order. This is the reassertion that what is being watched is a film and not reality. Reality (that of the real world) is neutralised so that reality (the created world order and the psychic reality of orders such as fantasy) can take place. The 'paranoid dialectic of identification' that emerges from the hysteric can be manipulated to describe the spectator, for this is precisely what takes place when we watch a film. Note that this is not simply the identification with a character, but rather the dialectic is between the actual spectator, the ideal spectator constructed by the film, the objects of the film (which will include characters), the cinematic apparatus (which will include the transpositional aspects of intertextuality, other film memories, and so on), the filmic culture (where the film is watched, under what conditions, with what responses and sensations).

But why see this as paranoid here? For Lacan's version this suits the hysteric – it is part of the symptom formation. Can we include this in the version of the spectator at hand? It is important to recall that for Freud a fundamental aspect of paranoia is its relationship to identification through the ideal ego.[67] It is this ideal ego that presents itself during the process of becoming a spectator, and this ultimately becomes the source of identification. The identification with the objects (in which we include people/actors as characters) in a film is mediated by the ideal ego as it makes the comparisons between the self and what is taking place. This is part of the reason why we see the spectator as a type of neurosis. And it is because of this function of the ideal ego that this relationship of the spectator to the objects in the film (and the totality of these objects as the film itself) can be seen as one of paranoia held, as it were, in abeyance. This returns us to the opening point of this quote – for in such a structure of the spectator we find the pursuit of knowledge. This is the desire to know formulated through lack and desire. What this knowledge is, and how it relates to madness and cinema, will be the concern of the next chapter.

CHAPTER 6

The Limits of Knowledge

The dog over us

What are the limits of knowledge? Where do we find that moment when knowledge collapses and its otherness is found? And what would we find beyond such limits, beyond knowledge and meaning? Madness will test knowledge to its limits; not just what is known and knowable, but how some things become located as knowledge. This is one of the forces of madness, of how it contests understanding and meaning, of its resistances to knowledge. For, in this force of madness, we find knowledge's Other and a construction of knowledge outside itself. This is because madness declares knowledge in its processes of non-meaning and makes systems of knowledge question themselves. For, in madness, knowledge is not so much negated, but rather tested and questioned. Its limits are found through the processes of challenging those aspects that allow knowledge to stand. And let us not forget, or underestimate, the productive side of that which exists outside of knowledge. In the force of madness a demand to be known emerges, a demand to develop understanding. A simple anecdote will serve to illustrate this. Freud 'realises/discovers/invents' (what word can suffice here?) the superego when one of his patients said to him 'I feel a dog over me' (*je sens un chien sur moi*).[68] This bizarre, seemingly nonsensical utterance became the foundation for a key element in psychoanalytic theory and the contemporary frame of mind. For Freud, it is not only this individual who feels a dog over them, it is all of us. From an utterance of seeming madness emerges a concept about consciousness itself. And such a dog becomes the test for knowledge. Of course, with this particular example, the testing of the limit produces a new form of knowledge.

To explore these ideas on knowledge and its limits we shall take up three related approaches. Firstly, a consideration of the challenge to interpretation and interpretative systems that madness performs, viewing it as part of a contesting of knowledge (both its formation and operation). This would include the proposition that there is something in cinema that allows for a sense of the otherness to knowledge (that is, that which is known). Secondly, the idea that cinematic knowledge can operate (sometimes *in potentia*) as a type of contestation to knowledge in much the same way that madness does, or has been positioned as possibly doing. Thirdly, the idea that there is a relationship between truth and knowledge that is founded on, and participates in, madness.

The challenge to interpretation

We are sliding over a complex question here. This is the question of 'what is the difference between interpretation and knowledge?' Sliding, because there is too much to take on here – a beyondness to our direct cinematic concerns; besides, we can afford a certain luxury of brevity for our real interest lies in what disturbs the sense of both knowledge and interpretation. At one level, the difference would seem to be something we do (interpret) as distinct from something we have (to know something); or something we do in order to achieve knowledge. There is a certain dialecticism here – we interpret in order to arrive at some point of knowledge, but we start from a standpoint of knowledge in order to achieve our interpretation. So Knowledge – – – Interpretation produces Knowledge that leads to further Interpretation, and so on. There are certain elements that will sustain such a cycle – new points of knowledge can reinforce an interpretation, just as interpretative gestures can strengthen a sense of knowledge. There are also elements that can disturb the cycle – new knowledge and/or interpretations can challenge the order of things.[69] When this takes place, even if the new ideas are in total contradiction to the established ones, the proposition of knowledge and the system of interpretation hold.

Madness disturbs, perhaps even arrests, the cycle in a different way. This presupposes that madness and knowledge are not different typologies but rather of the same order – a presupposition that is a direct legacy of the Freudian revolution. One of Freud's most profound contributions is the idea that the rational, civilised person is driven by an unconscious that deals in madness, and that to the conscious mind is madness. This is the psychopathology of everyday life; it is the interpretative gestures towards dreams as the royal road to the unconscious, it is the return of the repressed, it is parapraxis. In short, it is the idea that madness, in the version of the unconscious, defines our subjectivity, our cultural orders, our production of knowledges. And this is where we encounter Lacan. The unconscious as/is the Other – a site of knowledge production and at the same time unknowable in itself. What Freud gives (that is, we need to know the unconscious), it sometimes seems that Lacan takes away (that it is unknowable)!

Let us take a relatively simple aspect of this, commencing with this doubled/doubling question: how do we recognise knowledge? How do we arrive at the proposition that something is madness? How is one thing seen to be meaningful and another meaningless? And to work through some of the strands of this we can use, as metaphor and exemplar, some films. Our aim is a conflation of at least two different approaches: we are looking to unravel some of the relational aspects of knowledge and madness; we are aiming to use cinema as a method to do this. Cinema thus becomes an interpretative discourse to produce knowledge about knowledge. This is in contrast to what follows, when we will be looking to see how much cinematic knowledge mirrors madness as it actually disturbs the structures and formulations of knowledge. Such an inversion works because at the heart of all this is the sense that the destabilising of knowledge, through madness, is a necessary part of interpretation and meaning. Knowledge's Other – madness – is necessary because it provides the potential to see knowledge outside of itself.

How do we recognise knowledge? At one level, knowledge declares itself as such, it demands the status and calls for itself to be known. Certainly there are whole series of contextualising moments that point to a signifying process to be read as knowledge. Some of these are precursory, alerting us to the idea that what follows is knowledge; some are derived from the authority of the source; some are acts of faith, and so on. Such contexts orientate and organise interpretation in certain ways, but have the common task of making it a confirming act for the knowledge given. There is, for example, the cinematic convention of framing a film with declarative statements of truth and knowledge. These utterances and images occupy the paregonal logic of the frame, being neither inside (the film or the events they describe) or outside. When the detective stands and addresses the camera directly in the opening scene of *Summer of Sam* (Spike Lee 1999) and tells us that the following film is based on real events in New

York in 1977, we are predisposed to interpret things in certain ways. We will attribute a different status of knowledge to things according to this address, including our own knowledge of things such as American history, the events that took place at that time and place, Spike Lee films, cinematic conventions, and narrative devices. The knowledge such an address by the detective gives is about the ranges of knowledge that the film develops and can be located – from the events derived from real occurrences to the fictitious stories of the group of Italian-Americans. One of the interesting aspects of this particular example is that a certain type of relationship between knowledge and interpretation informs all the events in the film. From the knowledges of infidelity by the characters to the news footage (of riots, heat waves, sporting events), there is a constant slippage between the representation of real events and the created world order. Bonding this is the madness of the Son of Sam, whose acts of murder are shown to cause or bring to the fore paranoia, homophobia, xenophobia, racism, and sexual mistrust. It is madness that tests the limits of knowledge within the film – from the literal testing of not know-ing who the killer is and the evocation of violent, mad acts within the community, through to the spectator's own testing of knowl-edge as the film moves between real events and created worlds of narrative.

Compare this to something like *Memento* (Nolan 2000) where the knowledge from the past, inscribed on the body of Leonard Shelby and in notes to himself, is provided to give stability to inter-pretation. Yet, it is precisely the fluidity of the past events recalled as knowledge that makes interpretation impossible, or at least exceedingly difficult. The notes should occupy the site of knowl-edge, should convey that which is known and therefore beyond interpretation, but their limits are tested because of the sense of madness – the madness of continual forgetting and subsequent paranoia. A different use of the past as a type of knowledge occurs in *Shadow of the Vampire* (E. Elias Merhige 2000). Here we witness the fictional world order merge with the enacting of the making of *Nosferatu* so that this film stands in for a sense of truth about the earlier film. That a film called *Nosferatu* was made by Murnau in 1922 and has been seen by the spectator (that is, functions as a type of knowledge about cinema) displaces a different sense of knowledge into *Shadow of the Vampire*. The idea that *Nosferatu* has an actual vampire playing the role of a vampire can be seen as a metaphor for what cinema itself attempts to do. That is, a reality pretending to be a simulacra pretending to be a reality.

These three films show a certain cinematic attitude (which is derived from a broader cultural attitude) towards knowledge and the past. This is a model of the return of the repressed – that which is known to us, repressed but not forgotten. It is a type of knowledge that tests our interpretative powers, as Freud so deftly shows, because it is encased in disguise and repression. The desire to know this knowledge is tempered by our capacity, perhaps even our willingness, to confront what it means and what the consequences are. Vinny's wife, Dionna, in *Summer of Sam* represses the knowledge of his infidelities, but the culture of mistrust caused by the spiraling murders of the Son of Sam killer brings this knowledge back to her continually until she must act on it. (All of this is shown within a Catholic-driven culture of sexual conflict made up of Madonna-defined wives, and the sinful aspect of divorce, and certain sexual practices, such as fellatio, that are held as disrespectful to the status of a wife). So knowledge can be repressed, but will constantly return in an epistemologically-driven version of *Fort/da*.

Part of the reason such returns, and contesting, of knowledge can take place is that there has been set in place an attitudinal orientation of interpretation. Certain aspects of this are derived from a type of good knowledge/bad knowledge, with bad knowledge needing to be repressed. Of course, the status of good and bad will fluctuate – the notes in *Memento* are written as good knowledge but are often subsequently read as bad (that is, unstable, open to misinterpretation, connected to painful events, and so forth). There is also the imperative nature of some knowledges – they are positioned as essential to know, vital to the unraveling of the mystery or survival of those who ask the question. Thus 'Rosebud', for all its emptiness as knowledge, must be known; Kurtz in *Apocalypse Now* (Coppola 1979), for all his madness, must be known. This suggests that there is also a type of knowledge that declares itself as such, but does not necessarily come to any point of meaning. This is one of the attributes of the knowledge in madness – it seems meaningful, but what those meanings are will always be suspect.

There is a sense of Wittgenstein here, particularly of his work in relation to Freud. For although he had a problematical relationship with Freud, Wittgenstein never doubted the need to engage in these ideas, as when he states: 'having oneself psychoanalysed is like eating from the tree of knowledge. Knowledge acquired sets us (new) ethical problems; but contributes nothing to their solution' (Wittgenstein 1978: 34). What we sense is a type of knowledge that also looks like the imperative knowledge from films. The knowledge doesn't always contribute to its own solutions, but it does appear as knowledge.[70] Of course this is the other difficulty – the discourse of madness (like dreams) will always seem portentous. Just as cinema can set up signifiers to have doubled meaning (that is, the signifier has a meaning; at the same time it declares that this is a meaningful signifier – we are thinking of the sustained close-up as an example of this), so madness looks to have meaning and seem meaningful. At the same time madness undermines the whole process of meaning and interpretation and threatens to collapse in on itself.

The function of madness in the limits of knowledge operates within this compulsion of the need to know. It is encased in actions of desire and often has within it a sense that not to know this madness is to risk missing something essential. And no matter how unsatisfying the knowledge produced from this madness may be, we continue to pursue it because it is one of the most compelling forms of promissory resolutions. Here is one of the ironies of the relationship between madness and knowledge. Knowledge sets itself against madness, and yet one of the most compulsive formulations of knowledge is nothing less than madness itself. Once we have the sureties of certain types of knowledge (usually produced within our cultural contexts), once their limits have been negotiated and set, it is up to madness to disrupt within them and seduce beyond them. And here we witness part of cinema's function as a type of madness that tests these limits; for cinema can (but does not always it must be said) produce a knowledge outside of the knowledge that is known. Furthermore, it can participate in the drive to a beyond of the limits of knowledge. This is what has been argued throughout this study – that cinema and madness share this feature of producing a type of knowledge that cannot be dismissed, cannot be ignored, but in its very existence challenges meaning and interpretation.

It is perhaps no coincidence that one of the ways in which madness tests the limits of knowledge is through the subversive qualities of the sexual. The sexual is an aporia that constantly resists all forms of knowledge, and yet carries within itself a sense of knowledge. What Foucault nominates as the repressive hypothesis demonstrates precisely this process. In the first volume of *The History of Sexuality* (1984), Foucault describes how at the end of the nineteenth century there was an explosion of discourses on sexuality that had the effect of attempting to control it and keep it within certain relationships of power.[71] The variety of discourses produced positioned sexuality as something to be constrained, in effect something to be owned. This is part of the power/knowledge process – the production of discourses that determine knowledge within a managing process of power. And sex becomes the perfect cause for such discourse production because it is, like madness, a beyond to knowledge and therefore a threat to the power of knowledge. This is also part of the reason why sexuality and madness are so often linked together. As we have noted earlier, the hysteric resists knowledge through sexuality, and resists the positionality of sexual discourses (heterosexuality for example) through an otherness of knowledge.[72]

Lacan sees sexuality entangled in these aspects of knowledge and, of course, within his field of producing knowledge (that is, psychoanalysis) sexuality becomes both an object and methodology. For example, just when he leads us to the point of *serait science* (the 'would be science'/'would like to be science') (Lacan 1975: 76) so as to show us a difference to scientific discourse (which produces a sense of knowledge unlike any other), he then speaks of a subversion of knowledge and its link to sexuality. (Lacan 1975: 76, 1998: 82). The further tension within all this, from Foucault to Lacan, is precisely the interplay between knowledge and sexuality, and discourse, power and knowledge. How does one produce a discourse of sexuality without replicating a form of knowledge that has allegiance to the repressive discourses? Madness would seem to be one answer; and within that cinema is another. Not all cinema of course, for much of the cinematic process participates within the repressive discourses of curtailing sexuality, making it conform to what knowledge wants it to look like. But some films, and so by implication cinema as a cultural form, can perform this resistance, can offer a beyond to the limits of knowledge through the sexual. The significant thing to recognise about such cinematic examples is that what gives them this sense of resistance is as much the historical and cultural contexts (of both film and spectator) as to what they actually enact. The films of Pasolini, Jarman, Borowczyk (although perhaps only the earlier ones of this last example) spring to mind as having a type of knowledge derived from sexuality that tests the limits; but the examples may not always appear so 'extreme'. Subversion, of knowledge itself, is based on surprise and the force of differing, and this is not something that is easily codified. The images and narratives do not have to be excessive, explicit, or simply shocking to fulfill this contesting of knowledge through sexuality.

Cinema, knowledge and exceeding pleasure

This relationship between madness and sexuality, at the literal, representational level as well as at a more abstract, epistemological one, also illustrates how the limits of knowledge function across boundaries. The 'polymorphous techniques of power' (Foucault 1984: 11) must be able to make sense – that is, seem to produce meaning – within a range of disciplines in order to remain effective. The knowledge about sexuality (from the scientific to the *serait science*, to the historical, aesthetic, and so on) meets sexuality's knowledge, meets madness' knowledge, and finds resistance to its power. Cinema locates itself in both camps – as part of the polymorph of power where it contributes to the curtailment and repression of forms and representations of sexuality beyond the accepted discourses; and as part of the resistance to these through madness. In doing so, cinema exists in a continual state of possible madness, and its spectators find themselves in a constant state of possible resistances to the other discourses of knowledge. Here we have the *jouissance* of cinema and what it is to become a spectator within and through the cinematic apparatus. Such a proposition gives us the opportunity to consider further the shifting status of knowledge, truth, and subversion. This time we shall take up a model of four discourses that Lacan proposes in order to investigate relationships between subjectivity, knowledge, and truth. More significantly, he is concerned with how it is possible to challenge the systems of knowledge and the production of truth. Our concern will be to fit cinema, as a site of contestation, into such a model – particularly in regard to the position offered by Lacan to the hysteric.

In *L'Envers de la psychanalyse* (1991), Lacan creates the four discourses – four beautifully constructed models that operate with a sense of revolving relationships in order to denote different effects. The four elements of these models are:

$ – the *ichspaltung*. This is the split subject (*ich* = I; *Spaltung* = rupture, cleavage) and refers directly to a Freudian legacy. Lacan sees it as both an inevitable and problematic formation of the self. It is based on the idea that subjectivity is based on an irreparable split within the self as the subject moves through the Symbolic order. It is combined with the self-reflexivity of the Imaginary, originating as it does from the Mirror stage.

a – the *objet petit a*.[73] This is the manifestation of desires as they are articulated through the subject's relationship to otherness. Significantly, Lacan calls this the *Plus-de-Jouir*, which suggests a knowledge of *jouissance* emerging from the *objet petit a*. It also suggests a beyond to pleasure, particularly that inscribed by the cultural order.

S1 – master signifiers. At one level these are the signifiers of power and presence that have been developed in the Symbolic order. Thus they carry with them connotations of truth, knowledge, interpretation, and so on. These are also the signifiers that the subject has invested a sense of the self in. They are the discursive processes that allow the subject to relate to the signifiers, and for the signifiers to have meaning and relevance for the subject. In this way they become an essential component in the relationship of the defining of the self through the Other.

S2 – the systems of knowledge. This includes the sense of knowledge we might normally associate with such a term, and other interpretations of knowledge that the subject, and his/her Symbolic order, construct and are constructed by other systems. Because they are systems there is a sense of a shared (that is, cultural) basis of knowledge, although it would also be possible to locate something as unique as Shreber's interpretation of events as a system of knowledge. In other words, it is important not to conflate these with notions of truth, even if that is precisely what they come to stand for.

To these four elements Lacan specifies four positions:

$$\frac{d\acute{e}sir}{v\acute{e}rit\acute{e}} \qquad \frac{Autre}{perte}$$

(Lacan 1975: 106)

These can be translated as desire, Other, truth, and loss (or, perhaps more correctly, the production of loss).[74] These positions within the model later become attributed with certain qualities:

$$\frac{agent}{vérité} \qquad \frac{travail}{production}$$

(Lacan 1975: 196)

These are positions of agency, work, truth, and production. That which is located within the top left hand position is active and desired; below that is the site of truth (about which Lacan pointedly states: '*Quelle est la vérité? C'est bien là qu'elle se place, avec un point d'interrogation*' (Lacan 1975: 199). In admitting as much he seems to reflect his own uncertainty about such a position). The location of the top right is a positioning process – it is what the subject is interpellated into; and the bottom right is the resulting status of the subject who has allowed themself to be in a relationship with the factors on the left.

Now for the four discourses themselves:

The discourse of the university

$$\frac{S_2}{S_1} \quad \frac{a}{\$}$$

For Lacan, the discourse of the university commences with the agency of the system of knowledge, and the subject as an other of that system. This, then, is a highly systematic production of knowledge as knowledge. We are, as subjects, born into the existing Symbolic order, defined by the signifiers (of knowledge, of declared truths and meanings) that precede us. The discourse of the university operates as if there is an ideal I, full of mastery and control; and in doing so fails to eliminate this from the place where it finds its truth (Lacan 1975: 70–1). In other words, a very specific sort of truth is constructed – one which fits in with the production of (cultural) knowledge. (It is a discourse that Lacan defines himself as being, and working, outside of). It is noteworthy that in the graphic representation we find the left-hand side dominated by the system of knowledge and the master signfiers; the right hand side is composed of the subject as *objet petit a* and as a split subject.

The discourse of the master

$$\frac{S_1}{\cancel{S}} \quad \frac{S_2}{a}$$

This is the discourse that demands the relinquishing of a great many things. It demands total acceptance of the master signifiers as they interpret and define. Here the relationship between the master signifiers and the systems of knowledge places the *plus-de-jouir* – the excess and pleasure – in a suppressed position. Lacan states: '*le discours du maître exclut le fantasme*' (Lacan 1991: 124) – that is, Lacan's recurring formula of $S \lozenge a$.[75] The discourse of the master is a powerful and pervasive element in a great deal of our lives – it is also a tyrannical one. Lacan asks: '*Mais comment l'arrêter, ce petit mécanisme?*' (Lacan 1991: 207). Not through revolution because, argues Lacan, that is simply a perpetuation of the discourse, or at the very least of the relationships within the discourse. Rather the way to stop or escape this is through the discourse of the analyst.

So far we have two discourses that position themselves as absolute producers of knowledge and truth. The certainty of institutionalised knowledge (the discourse of the university) and the excluding acts of the master signifiers are part of their constitution. Lacan proposes two alternatives to these discourses, two systems that operate outside of the absolutism of these other two. These are the discourses of psychoanalysis and the hysteric, and it is the latter that concerns us the most here.

The discourse of the hysteric

$$\frac{\cancel{S}}{a} \quad \frac{S_1}{S_2}$$

In the discourse of the hysteric we observe that the primary position – the top left hand side – is occupied by the split subject. The *ichspaltung* is the subject type that has been repressed in the discourses of the master and the university. This is a site of resistance against the master signifiers (that is, those that stand for unquestioned/unquestionable truth) and the established discourses of knowledge; and in this way we read the structure of $\cancel{S}/a$ as a distinct area *contra* S_1/S_2. This becomes clearer if we refer to comments by Lacan in the seminar entitled *The Psychoses*. In this he states: 'What is repression for the neurotic? It's a language, another language that he manufactures with his symptoms, that is, if he is a hysteric or an obsessional, with the imaginary dialectic of himself and the other. The neurotic symptom acts as a language that enables repression to be expressed' (Lacan 1993: 60). In such a model, then, the hysteric is the one who resists the powers of systems of knowledge and the dominance of the master signifiers. And this takes place not necessarily as a revolutionary act, but because he/she is defined, that is their subjectivity is defined, through the manifestation of the repressed material. That which cannot be expressed in discourses dominated by the master signifiers and the institutions of knowledge (in this case the example given by Lacan is the university) becomes the voice in the discourse of the hysteric. And such discourses necessarily produce a different sort of language because so much of what is expressed cannot be represented in the discourses of institutionalised knowledge and master signifiers.

Cinema as madness can be placed, and can be seen to operate, within the discourse of the hysteric in a number of ways. Graphically it is rendered as:

$$\frac{\$ - \text{Cinema-Spectator}}{a - \text{excess } jouissance} \qquad \frac{S_1 - \text{master signifiers as other}}{S_2 - \text{knowledge as production/loss}}$$

Cinema, and its demands on the formation of the spectator, occupies the site of desire and agency as the force of cleavage. Cinema splits the subject through all those apparatus that have been discussed so far – the issues of truth and knowledge, the inmixing of realities, the mirroring of neurosis and psychosis, alienation and identification, and so on. And this is done, significantly, through desire – cinema becomes the site of desire, the spectator becomes the subject of desire. Such desires themselves force splits, as cinema and spectator produce images of desire that can run counter to the Symbolic. This leads us to the second part of this formulation, where the site of truth in the cinematic experience is occupied by excess and *jouissance*. This is the potential, excessive pleasures of the combined cinema and spectator. The domain of truth becomes the *plus-de-jouir*, exceeding anything that attempts to represent it. This is the representation of the impossible, exemplified in the attempts to represent madness outside of itself, but found within all cinematic experiences. This position of truth as *jouissance* means that any discursive element of cinema is always returned to an impossible signification of excess and disruption through the acts of the spectator.

The master signifiers (S1) are othered not as sites of desires (the impossibility of truth for example) within cinema, but as questioned statements in themselves. In this way, it is not desire that seems distinct from the spectator, but knowledge. This is the contradictory status of knowledge in cinema; of how we, as spectators, correlate cinematic realities with other forms of reality. It is significant in this regard that phantasy, such a fundamental element in the discourse of the hysteric, and so profoundly excluded in the discourse of the Master, is an intricate part of this cinematic knowledge. The systems of knowledge themselves are located within a site of the production, but also of loss – that is, a systematic production of knowledge is also the production of loss. As with hysteria (and neurosis, and so forth, for Lacan does not limit this model to the hysteric), cinema and its spectators are sites for the resistance to master signifiers because those signifiers are seen as inadequate in the representation of the subject and desire. Such signifiers are incapable of handling the repressed material, and this becomes the function of cinema. This is why elements of pure phantasy can occupy exactly the same site and sit alongside those produced from reality. In the discourses of the Master and the University, phantasy is excluded so that 'reality' can have a sense of the master signifier (and, by implication and effect, the master signifiers become invested in reality); whereas in the discourse of the hysteric and cinema (although obviously there are some differences between these two) phantasy becomes another version of reality, and vice versa. If this is the case, and those elements traditionally seen as the sites of truth and knowledge (the master signifiers and institutions of knowledge) are contested and undermined, the question then becomes what is the relationship of the cinematic discourse, organised through the excess *jouissance* as truth, to the split subject/spectator as agency? And where do we position knowledge within such an arrangement? This is the line we must now explore further.

Cinematic knowledge and madness

What has been at stake so far here is the relationship between the discourses that produce knowledge and those that are figured as madness. Or, put another way, the movement towards that which is seen as meaning(ful) and that which resists meaning but is not meaningless. The relationships that exist are crucial to the survival of both – knowledge needs its limits tested, and the resistances need to be seen as potentially meaningful. The type of knowledge that cinema produces can be of both orders, but there is a compulsion to see it as a knowledge that is known or at least can be known. This is, in part, because all narrativised systems present themselves as having some sort of meaning (this is one of the functions of narrative). It is also in part because attached to cinema are various types of knowledge that are used to make meaning within it and from it. These would include specific cinematic knowledges (such as theories of montage, lighting, narrative, genre, diegetics, and so on) as well as the broader ones related to cultural and historical aspects. If enough of these types of knowledges surround and permeate the cinematic object then no matter how great the enigmatisation, no matter how much it resists meaning, the spectator will always pursue a sense of knowledge and meaning. Although, what we argue here is that this is more in keeping with the disruptive knowledge of the hysteric than within the institutionalised frames that cannot contain the excesses of cinema.

Let us now consider further the ideas on cinematic knowledge as a type of madness. This, in some ways, runs counter to what we observed in the first part of this section. Yet, any sense that the knowledges that cinema produces somehow operate as types of madness can only really be articulated if there is a companion sense of such knowledges as having meaning within the Symbolic order. The mad knowledge of cinema can be seen as part of the larger order of madness that functions to resist, provoke, and often to be enjoyed. This is the explosive delights of pleasure, where solution gives way to play and disruption. It exists to unsettle and cajole. This is the relationship of knowledge to *jouissance*. Such an idea finds a home in the work of Lacan, whose final seminars cover some of this. At one point Lacan states: 'Yet the crux of or the key to what I put forward this year concerns the status of knowledge, and I stressed that the use of knowledge could but imply a *jouissance*' (Lacan 1998: 137). Lacan's line of thought throughout this seminar (significantly subtitled *The Limits of Love and Knowledge*) is how we might read the unconscious as a producer of knowledge, that there is a certain type of knowledge that belongs to the unconscious. Interestingly, but beyond our direct concerns here, he positions love as the other type of knowledge involved.[76] For Lacan, psychoanalysis becomes the discourse capable of reading such a knowledge – or at least this should be the aim of psychoanalysis – and this is the foundation for the fourth discourse model (the discourse of the analyst). The types of issues raised in such a project have direct interest for a reading of cinema knowledge. For this type of knowledge presents many similarities with the knowledge from the unconscious, particularly in terms of madness.

One connection is *jouissance*, which here stands for the disruptive pleasures of knowledge against meaning. In one version, this is the aligning of desire/agency in the rent/split subject and the objects of desire in the site of truth, placed oppositionally to the master signifiers of knowledge and other forms of knowledge as loss. There is another, related sense to this, where the relationship of the excesses of pleasure broker the subject's position and reality. For it is important to realise that this is not to imply that *jouissance* exists outside of meaning or even reality. As Lacan formulates 'Reality is approached with apparatuses of *jouissance*' (Lacan 1998: 55). How curious this is! Here we see those elements – desire, excessive pleasures, the socially disruptive, pleasure and delight – normally associated with a loss of reality now forming the subject's relationship to reality. Rather than providing the escape from reality, acts of *jouissance* become integral parts of it. What, then, is this relationship of knowledge and cinema as it appears as madness and out of the disruptive moment of *jouissance*? Let us take a number of propositions on this:

• Cinema knowledge is always tinged with *jouissance*
This must be so because this is part of the pleasure of cinema. It contributes to the compulsive, attractive attributes of being a film spectator, it is why we go and watch films. Here knowledge flows both ways – when we become a spectator we have knowledge of the *jouissance* that comes with the film (this is part of the reason we watch films, it is part of the pleasure of being a spectator, and it is part of the incitement to become a spectator); and we bring to the film a certain type of anticipatory *jouissance*. This is one of the processes in the formation of the spectator as a version of neurosis and psychosis. This is so because the tinge of *jouissance* that cinema knowledge has, that it must always produce in some form and to some extent, is one that is conflictual with reality. Note that this is

conflictual, which requires the holding together of the dispersive
elements, and not necessarily a schism. And because *jouissance* is an
excessive pleasure, a beyond to the culturally acceptable, any
meanings and knowledges produced out of it will contain the
excessive sensibilities of madness. This is where the knowledges of
madness and cinema are an overflow to the knowledges contained
within the socially constructed realities. They are, however, knowledges; and this has been one of the primary sites of contested
attributes. Cinema and madness possess and produce knowledges,
some of which are devised from the material of the repressed.

• Cinema knowledge emerges from the spectator
Cinema knowledge cannot be seen as something contained solely
within the film, emerging from it as if by osmosis or germination,
or even a flash of brilliance. It cannot be seen as a formula or list
of details. It must be a combination of elements, textual and extra-
textual, not the least being the formation of the spectator as
he/she creates the film in the viewing. This is the transpositional
flow of images and ideas from the film and all its images and
sounds, other films, the spectator's own knowledge of films, the
structures and interplay of cinematic knowledges (such as
montage, narrative). From such combinations comes knowledge
about that particular film being experienced at that particular
time, as well as a wider sense of knowledge that will come into play
when other films are watched.

The other aspect of this is that the sorts of knowledges that are
produced will vary immensely. So wide is this category that it must
include everything from the relatively straightforward (such as the
knowledge gained about the jump-cut and editing in *A bout de souffle*) to the highly abstract (the knowledge about knowledge, the
revelations of distinctions between truth and error, ideas on epistemophilia). Not everything is taken up by the spectator, however,
for there can be no guarantees in this production of knowledge.
And here we witness another parallel to the unconscious knowledge that concerns psychoanalysis. Just as the unconscious is articulated and manifested in various ways and is not heard or
understood, so the combination of spectator and film produces
layers of knowledge, not all of which are acted on, recognised, or
thought about. Some will emerge during a viewing, others in
subsequent viewings (if the film is watched again), others during
discussions and remembrances, and others will lie repressed, or

become part of the material of the unconscious itself. But this does not mean that they are not there, in continual states of production and reproduction. (It is not even too much to argue that this cinematic material becomes part of the formulation in dreams and phantasies as manifestations of the unconscious). Here, we note the similarity between the sorts of knowledges that the spectator produces from the film and Barthes' idea, in *The Pleasure of the Text* (1980), on the text of *jouissance*. In contrasting the text of pleasure – (the text 'that contents, fills, grants euphoria; the text that comes from culture and does not break with it' (Barthes 1988: 14) – with the text of *jouissance* – the text that 'imposes a state of loss, the text that discomforts' (Barthes 1988: 14) – Barthes emphasises the creative role of the reader (for us the spectator), as well as the disruptive crises that such a relationship brings.

- Cinema knowledge tests the limits of knowledge by confirming its own, and the spectator's, relationship to reality

As Lacan asserts, we negotiate reality through *jouissance* because, in the psychoanalytic field, this is the 'speech' of the unconscious. The same can be said of cinema – we, as spectators, approach the 'reality' of the created world order of a film through *jouissance*, as well as taking up the disruptive pleasures that the spectating position offers to us. As was argued before, this negates the idea that when we read a text or view a film, there must be a willing suspension of disbelief, and instead posits that even in the most escapist of films, the spectator is in fact renegotiating reality (which includes all systems of interpretation, ideologies, versions of truth) through his/her experiences of *jouissance*. So what is gained in the pleasures of cinema is an approach to reality via the apparatuses of *jouissance*. The implication is that cinema knowledge, through *jouissance*, produces a knowledge about reality – that is, other forms of knowledge. This is the assertion of madness within knowledge, not as a counter to that knowledge, but rather as a way of understanding it through its limitations.

It is clear that cinema knowledges are seen as distinct from other forms of knowledge, particularly the two large orders that we might term reality and the analytic. The first of these – reality – is seen as a knowledge (as well as a space for certain forms of knowledge) that is not to be confused with that of dreams, phantasy, fictions, stories, and of course films. Anyone who was to confuse reality and filmic reality would be seen as mad, and the greater the confusion the more extreme the madness. Schreber, with his psychosis to escape reality through the creation of an alternate one, is seen as an excess of madness that removes him from reality. Psychoanalysis judges someone like Schreber as an extreme version of madness because his submersion in the psychotic reality is so deep, so very difficult to penetrate. Similarly, analytic knowledge (that which is said to produce truths and analysis of reality, as well as those other realms such as dreams and texts) is seen to be of a particular type of truth-producing process. Yet what has been argued throughout this book is that cinema, like madness, produces knowledge that functions both as reality and outside of it. Similarly, it can also produce versions of analytic knowledge. This is not to say the metaphorical or allegorical manner (such as the representation and commentary on the cultural struggle in poverty in *Rome, Open City* (Rossellini 1946) can be said to produce a knowledge about Italy at the end of the Second World War, or of the fight against fascism), but as a status of knowledge itself. And how it does this is through resistances and contesting of limits, through the disruptions of *jouissance*, and through the seduction of the subject into the role of the spectator. For in that spectating position filmic reality produces a knowledge more real than reality, with at least as much, sometimes more, credibility and meaning. Because this is the spectator who cares; there is resonance in the act of watching the film.[77] Here, we witness the Hegelian watch, where a moment of error passes as truth, and truth later comes to be seen as error – but at the time of consideration all we know is a sense of reality. This brings us to the third part of our enquiry.

Truth and knowledge out of madness

Let us return to the idea of resistance, of a resistance that enigmatises. This is a resistance to knowledge, but not all knowledge, only certain types. It is also a resistance to analysis that may well prove to be unresolvable. In other words, here is a form of resistance that exists to be counter to analysis, to test knowledge. This is the third part of the equation for us here. The first being that cinema can produce, and has, knowledge beyond itself; the second being that cinema knowledge, like unconscious knowledge (that is, knowledge from the unconscious), engages in reality through *jouissance* and the formation of the spectator; the third, this one, is that the impossibility of analysing certain aspects (signifiers[78]) conclusively is part of cinema knowledge. What this suggests is that a part of the function of cinema's knowledge is to provide resistance to the idea (born, in some ways for the contemporary world, from the Enlightenment) that every problem has a solution, that all analysis can be refined to become better at solving the enigmas. We have returned to the Freudian navel, where the realisation that there are some things that analysis cannot untangle is seen not as a limitation, but as an insight into these other forms of knowledge. As Derrida puts it, from a different context, all resistances have a meaning within themselves which may well be independent of the point of the analysis: 'resistance not only comprehended and communicated in its *intelligibility*, but transformed, transposed, transfigured. At stake, then, are sense and truth' (Derrida 1998: 18).[80]

Sense and truth. For sense to operate in a film the spectator must adhere to, and participate in the construction of, truths within the reality of the film. But to do this he/she must do away with (put in suspension, in abeyance, as the phenomenologists would say) the notions of sense and truth that operate in the real world. This is one of the first, most primary, forms of a resistance beyond analysis that cinema provides. For a spectator to be, for a film to exist, sense and truth must bend. This is not simply to say that a film makes sense within itself, and that the truths it produces within its created world order remain constant within themselves. More than this, cinema comes to be part of the same resistances that madness provokes. This is not to deny the large part of cinema that exists within the hegemonic processes of a culture, or to deny the role that cinema plays in the sustaining of various cultural discourses of power/knowledge (including the normalising of the sexual, notions of discipline and restraint, various versions of repression, curtailment of excess, a buttress for ethical orders). Beyond these, however, cinema exists *in potentia* as mad resistance, as part of the discourse of the hysteric who develops knowledge out of desire and rupture. To paraphrase Derrida (who was, in fact, referring to literature), there is no cinema, or very little cinema – the sort of cinematic demand, via the formation of the spectator, that constantly provides resistances of this order. This is, as was noted in earlier discussions here, the hysterical version of the spectator who runs counter to the Good; the neurotic spectator who eroticises the filmic signifier; the psychotic spectator who transgresses versions of reality, and all that is contained in the permutations of these spectating positions.

We now need to note the difference between elements in a film that resist analysis (for any length of time), and those elements in a film that are resistance in itself. Ultimately, it is this second type that is of primary interest here, because in them we make more connections with the motifs of madness. The first of these is the enigmatisation process – where a film (or even a whole group of films, such as the genres of *noir* and the thriller that has this process as part of its defining qualities) sets up sites that will resist initial attempts of interpretation. This can be based on those notions of truth and sense, for the resistance to analysis in these cases often stems from an inability to settle on a sense of the truth. The thing about these forms of resistance is that they are always false, and almost inevitably the films themselves provide the analytic moment of resolution. *The Sixth Sense* (M. Night Shyamalan 1996) and *Siesta* (Lambert 1987) reveal the analytic truth about the investigating character at the end of the narrative. Their initial (disguised) deaths are the moments of resistance to analysis, but become the key to understanding all the elements in the film once it is revealed. Similarly, Rosebud in *Citizen Kane* resists analysis, only to be revealed at the end; Roger 'Verbal' Kint in *The Usual Suspects* (Singer 1995) provides puzzles that are shown to have all their answers laid out in the background *mise-en-scène*. The final defeat of the alien in *Signs* (M. Night Shyamalan 2002) is performed through the combining of the signs for each of the four main characters. The baseball bat, the obsession with clean water, asthma, and faith are all positioned as signs of weakness as well as strength. These versions of supposed resistances in all these examples are actually part of the analytic tradition that argues that all resistances can be resolved. In their narrative solutions what is 'proven' is the strength of the analytic process. In this sense they are false resistances, and their pleasure rests in that what they present as enigma can, and will, be resolved. The disentangled solutions provide a bringing together of all the elements within the film.

The second order of resistances are the ones that appear to have no textual point of resolution, no possible disentanglement. In these films the enigmatising process seems to continue beyond the elements of the film itself. Surrealist cinema, some of Antonioni's films (the sorts of existentialist ideas of loss and lack of knowledge about the self found in *The Passenger* and *L'Avventura* (1960), for example, *Last Year at Marienbad*, even the conclusion of *Lost Highway* (Lynch 1997) and *Mulholland Drive*, fit into this category. These are not true resistances in the sense of the Freudian navel however, for even though we may not share a common understanding, or even have an easy sense of what they mean, what truths they hold or may produce, there are ways of reading them. As distinct from the first category, these resistances have their pleasure precisely in the lack of resolution, or in the instability of any posited resolutions.[80] These are versions of meaning that exceed the boundaries that cinema sets itself. If a film seems to lack coherent meaning, or exceeds meaning in its polysemic nature (that is, emphasises that a number of different readings can sit side-by-side), this is not necessarily an unresolvable resistance to analysis. What such elements in a film do suggest, in their proliferation of possible meanings, is that analytic work is needed.

The resistance to analysis that concerns Freud, that Derrida picks up on and describes as the hyperbolic resistances, that in a way Foucault celebrates in his Nietzschean formations of power/knowledge, and Lacan spends a lifetime both discovering and creating, eventually driving him to concepts such as the borromean knots and strings, is different from these other two types. It is the moment where the analyst recognises the absolute impossibility of working the analysis through to a satisfying conclusion, or for that matter any sort of conclusion. This is its meaning – to resist. And rather than being exemplified in any single film, we argue here that this is part of what makes cinema cinema, of what is entailed in becoming a cinematic spectator, of where particular types of pleasures of cinema itself reside. In this sense it is something that exists in all films, even if it is rarely apparent. This is the case not because of some sort of textual design or intent, but rather is the interplay between spectator and film within the various apparatus involved, including the cinematic, the cultural, the analytic. This attribute of resistance is also part of that which has come to be seen in/as madness.

The limits to meaning

Let us now return to an earlier question: how does something come to be seen as meaningful or meaningless at all? How does something which has the effect of meaning demand to be read as such? The difference between meaning in reality and meaning in madness can help us understand how meaning operates in cinema (and perhaps, although this might be somewhat of an impossible project, how cinema shows us something of the operation of meaning in reality and madness). We must write 'meaning in reality and meaning in madness' because there is a difference in meaning, of meaning, here. Madness operates as the otherness to meaning, interpretation, knowledge, and so on. And for much of its history the meaning of madness has been seen to lie in reality. From the supernatural, to the animality, to the theories of the humours and fluids, to the social, and to the unconscious motivations, to find the meaning of madness has meant to track it back to something that exists within the world order of reality. These elements that constitute explication of madness are unusual in that they must exist in the liminal zone between madness and reality. In other words they occupy reality and madness through their interpretative gestures. This is why ideas such as the return of the repressed, the somatic manifestations of mental disturbances in hysteria, the wish fulfillment nature of dreams, even the Oedipal complex and theories of sexuality – in short the vast foundations of psychoanalysis – at one level operate to track the symptoms of madness back to some part of reality. In such an interpretative model, reality becomes the source pool to give meaning to mad episodes, and at the same time madness is employed to make sense of versions of reality.

What becomes clear, however, is that the tracing back process is actually yet another construction. Freud's tracing back of Dora's hysterical symptoms to the scene beside the lake becomes part of *his* version of the reality of the events in her life. His reading of the kiss, and of Dora's desires for the kiss, are not really a tracing back to reality, but a tracing back to a reality constructed by Freud. This in turn becomes the mechanism of transference. The same can be said of what happens in cinema. We can take this at two levels: the literal representation of such tracing back; the relationship of cinema to reality. In the first of these we find the hermeneutic exercise of understanding how a narrative develops and of how its elements fit together. This is nowhere more apparent than in those genres where detecting and concluding drive the films themselves. So, for example, the tracing back of Norman Bates' acts to the 'reality' of events in his childhood, or the tracing back to the white past (which comes to constitute reality) of the daughters by Ethan in *The Searchers*. Here we witness a type of resolution compulsion, where the narrative demands a lineage to a previous time; this is the explication through a psychic and/or socio-cultural history. Beyond such representations is the wider implication that cinema constantly sets up an apparatus of tracing back to reality. The more obvious example is documentary, but the same can be said of totally fictitious films. What all such models of tracing back reveal is a sense of meaning lying somewhere beyond the text, to these elements that exist between reality and non-reality (which is figured here as madness). At the heart of this are the construction of meaning and the primacy of the interpretation. Yet there is also a meaning in madness that goes beyond this tracing back. How such contesting of meanings distorts the inventions of meaning and interpretation can be illustrated by a story from Lacan.

In a seminar entitled 'The Hysteric's Question', Lacan recounts a case study by Joseph Eisler (Lacan 1993: 168) of a Hungarian tram conductor. The account took place at the end of the First World War, which is significant, less for its sense of historical and social closure and more for the changes in the relationships of technology to the self. It seems that one day there was an accident on the tram, and this conductor slipped and was dragged a short distance. He was taken to hospital and, after a thorough examination, the doctors declared him fit and well. They took a lot of x-rays and were certain of their diagnosis, arguing that he was putting on an act. However, the tram conductor kept complaining about pains in his side, continually acting as if in a great deal of physical discomfort, and eventually reaching a state where he would black out. After another round of examinations, where again nothing physically wrong was found, the doctors sent him to Eisler as they suspected a traumatic hysteria.

Eisler documents his sessions with the tram conductor, recounting a number of instances of what he sees as particular behaviours of transference. Eisler focuses on the anal character of the tram conductor's actions and, in particular, what he sees as a homosexualising tendency. For him, this is the source of the trauma, but, as Lacan points out, this leads him nowhere in terms of solving the anguish of the subject.

Lacan offers a different reading – a quite ingenious reading really. He begins by considering the traumas of the conductor and Eisler's interpretations of them. Lacan argues against Eisler's interpretation of regression and negation, and instead posits that the onset of trauma wasn't the accident of falling from the tram at all, but rather it was the radiographic examination. It is during the examinations 'which subject him to mysterious instruments that the subject's crises are triggered' (Lacan 1993: 170). Furthermore, these crises are not simply about an anal drive or homosexual identities, rather they are about formations of subjectivity in the Symbolic order; the breakdown 'isn't Imaginary but Symbolic' (Lacan 1993: 213) (translation modified). Here we witness Lacan performing a different sort of tracking back for the explication of the madness; not to childhood events but of the terrors of a new technology and their position in the cultural events (that is, post First World War with its technologically-derived mass deaths). The conceptual frame of interpretation, that the aspects of madness are meaningful, is never questioned, nor is the need to trace it back to some form of reality (childhood and social events). Meaning, then, is seen to exist both within the madness and outside of it. This is part of the reason why madness occupies such a curious, paregonal position in terms of meaning and knowledge. As is the case with this story, and all moments of madness, no matter what version of interpretation is taken up, the hysteric's questions remain as part of a contesting of what constitutes truth and meaning.

Cinema, like madness, has these polymorphic and paregonal attributes of meaning. At one level, aspects of it can be tracked back to reality – we make sense of a great deal of a film in its relationship to reality (the simulacra, mimesis, and all those versions of connections and replications). It is also tracked back to the Symbolic, that is, the cultural events and situations that films are derived from, as well as the cultural field in which they operate. This would include everything from narrative sequences (sense of history), gender roles, ideologies, systems of beliefs – in short the cultural order of things. Meaning is also made by tracking various elements and sequences back to the realities of the film itself (which includes, at some level, the realities of cinema as a textual and cultural system). Certain events take place in the film that become realities for all other events, and unless there is some reason given (such as a generic one in the case of supernatural or science fiction films), we expect these realities to be sustained. This is part of the third order of making meaning – individual films rely on meaning structures from the cinematic apparatus. Cuts, sound (both diegetic and non-diegetic), camera angles, lighting, and so forth all are meaning producing systems within a film because they have meaning beyond that film. There are also the meanings generated within the discourses of an individual film that will often remain unique to that film. Transpositional elements can carry meanings across films (an actor can have additional meanings because of the types of characters they are known to play; camerawork that is used in similar ways – the steadi-cam for example – generates meanings across films). All of these elements – and the others too numerous to mention – generate meanings and cause films to be seen as meaningful. They are different from the meanings generated out of cinema's relationship to reality (in, for example, the real events that *Summer of Sam* are based on, a documentary, live footage; the interplay devised by both film and spectator between Mureau's *Nosferatu* and the making of it, with the real vampire, in *Shadow of the Vampire*) because they are cinematic – and yet their function at the level of meaning shares the drive of rendering the sign to be seen as something meaningful. This takes place within the reality of the cinematic signifier and the role of the spectator of these signifiers.

The third source of meaning comes from the spectator. Most overtly, these are those particular elements in a film that become meaningful because of what we as spectators bring to them and attribute to them. But beyond this almost literal aspect is the idea that meaning is founded on such a relationship. This would be meaning generated out of desire. For Lacan this links it to the Imaginary: For him, there is no question that 'meaning is by nature imaginary. Meaning is, like the imaginary, always in the end evanescent, for it is tightly bound to what interests you, that is, to that in which you are ensnared' (Lacan 1993: 54). Madness, like cinema, illustrates this particularly well. The psychotic, for example, will find their reality of meaning, of interest in fact, because it is the most relevant structure for them. In this way, it is not reality that becomes meaningful, but that which is meaningful to the subject that becomes reality. More than this, it is the only reality they are capable of seeing. The cinematic spectator is the same – cinema is part of the Imaginary, and its meanings and pleasures are derived from what interests us as spectators. This is the difference between seeing a film as having meaning (the culturally inscribed) and being meaningful (derived from the spectator). This aspect of being derived from the spectator – what we take to the film and how we manipulate the realities of the film to fit within ourselves – finds a parallel in psychosis, here exemplified by

Schreber. As with psychosis, the spectator negotiates aspects of the reality he/she is experiencing (the real world, psychic reality, and cinematic reality, as well as the combinations of them) from the position of *jouissance*. This is the excessive pleasure of watching a film and becoming a spectator. How much this takes place will vary from film to film, spectator to spectator, just as is the case with psychosis. With Schreber this is quite extreme: Lacan's view of Schreber is a subject who is consumed by his delusions, so much so that they are the primary constitutive elements of reality. Schreber invests all of his surroundings, in totality, with the meaningfulness of his delusions. This is how the spectator views the film (or parts of a film) as meaningful. And it is delusional in as much it is invested with this sense of subjectivity and reality.[81]

These three primary components, no matter how diverse and broad they are seen, cannot account for all the matter of cinema. There are still aspects of meaning and meaninglessness that are beyond them. These are the excesses of meaning, the knot that cannot be untangled, the point where knowledge itself is challenged. How we actually recognise something as the challenge to meaning involves an interplay between the cultural order and our own Imaginary plane of existence. The difference between being culturally meaningful and having meaning for the spectator may not vary very much, but it is important that slippages can take place. The lines from Lacan cited above raise another aspect of this – the delusion of meaning. Such a phrase implies that something stands as meaningful and yet all it really has is the sense of meaning without actually being meaningful. Let us spend a moment comparing this to the function of meaning in cinema.

When a spectator recoils in fear at a frightening scene, cries in a moment of sadness (when a character dies or love is lost), becomes sexually aroused, laughs with nervousness or delight – when a spectator reacts to what is taking place in a film as if it is reality, is this a delusion of meaning? Can we argue that such reactions are meaningful in this delusional way, and that it is delusion itself that gives them meaning? This is the case with neurosis and psychosis – Schreber believes the delusions of his womanliness and the plots to kill him. He must or they would not be meaningful. This is in keeping with the ideas of cinema, madness, and the formation of the spectator. For what is at hand is not the idea that the spectator believes the reality of the image as if it is true. It is always a film; we always return to the point of created world orders and reality; we do not continue the created realities into the real world. But what he/she does believe, as a spectator, is that that reality (derived from those various sources of the cultural, textual, and psychical) has a meaning – is meaningful, is taken seriously. That it is the delusional quality that the spectator shares with madness.

In cinema, as with madness, the force of the reality created through the delusions is based on meaningfulness. And the cinema spectator, like the mad person, is the primary agent in creating this sense of meaning as they become immersed in the signifiers, the illusions and their passions. Certainly there are the culturally shared and constructed meanings and experiences; there are those elements that interpellate at the level of the social, including the ideological functions. There are also those that bond the group of spectators together. Yet none of this runs against the idea that primary to the act of spectating is this relationship of meaning, reality, and delusion. In this, we see madness and cinema and the pleasures of when the two entwine.

Notes

Chapter 1

1 By this, we intend all the aspects of cinema and not simply the films themselves. This would include, along with specific films, the cultural contexts, production, spectatorship, theorising methodologies. It is also inclusive of the most casual conversations and the most abstract theorising on films. It is the shared cultural knowledge of films, the historical development of cinema, the innovative and reactionary. It is also intended to mean the composite of all these elements in their unrealised forms.

2 See, for example, Wolfgang Iser *The Act of Reading*. These works have a literary agenda, but the idea of an implied spectator works just as well.

3 See Lacan 1993: 123.

4 It is worth recalling that for Foucault, with his detailed examinations of discursive practices, systems of statements, and the idea of power/knowledge, that a word such as *œuvre* will seldom be employed simply as 'work'. Note, for example, how the discussion of œuvre in the address 'On the Archaeology of the Sciences: Response to the Epistemological Circle' (Foucault 2000) encapsulates issues such as unity, opus, historical conditions, authorship, and interpretation.

5 As he puts it: 'In our time, the politico-religious meaning of festivals has been lost; instead, we resort to alcohol or drugs as a way of contesting the social order, and we have thus created a kind of artificial madness. Basically, it is an imitation of madness, and it can be seen as an attempt to set society ablaze by creating the same state as madness' (Foucault 2000: 340).

6 See the debate between them, especially the essays collected in Derrida's *Resistance*.

7 We acknowledge Barthes' models of pleasure and *jouissance*, of the readerly and writerly, of the *studium* and *punctum* within such a distinction.

Chapter 2

8 This is the famous exchange between Foucault and Derrida, instigated by *Madness and Civilization* (Foucault 1987), and then developed in Derrida's response 'Cogito and the History of Madness', Foucault's response in '"To Do Justice To Freud": The History of Madness in the

Age of Psychoanalysis'. We shall return to this debate later in this chapter.

9   This, of course, is Foucault's starting point in *Madness and Civilization*. He notes that the Middle Ages marks the point where madness becomes textualised, even if the origins of these stories are much older.

10   This sense of the big O Other is drawn from Lacan's idea of the order of otherness itself. It is distinct from the little o other, which can be seen as manifestations of this. In this sense the fears of the Other referred to here indicates not so much a specific fear/threat but a sense of fear from that order that contains all the possible others.

11   Consider such representations in Diderot, Rabelais, Swift – and back, further and further in time – to Aristophanes, Aristotle and Plato where other cultures are seen as madness and folly, where laughter becomes the defining frame. The function of such othering through madness is almost invariably to make one's own cultural habits seem more rationale and sane.

12   Here we find many of the themes and issues of the treatment and representation of hysteria. Freud's case study of Dora is revolutionary in its reflexivity and attempts to locate Dora's acts and thoughts within a different model of hysteria, and yet we still observe many of these issues of the family as both case and possible cure. The long history of hysteria – at least back to the ancient Egyptians – places this as a mental instability caused by women's sexuality and physiology. The idea of the family, and marriage, as a preventative for hysteria was particularly popular in the nineteenth century, and was only really dispelled through the work of Freud. It is interesting to note that a great deal of hysteria as shown in cinema seems to borrow from this pre-Freudian model. The women (and it was Freud who was one of the first to argue that not only women can be hysterical) in such films are often shown as outsiders to the family, envious of such a structure, desiring to be part of it. Although we do see this sense of the desired family in Travis Bickle.

13   Alfred Nettement, a nineteenth-century journalist, voiced the common sentiment that women should not be allowed to read novels for fear they would become over-passionate and even mad. In 1840 Marie Cappelle-Lafarge was put on trial for murdering her husband, inflamed, it was argued, because she had been reading *Les Mémoires du diable*, a novel by Frédéric Soulié. See Matlock *Scenes of Seduction* (1994) for details on this and other case histories in nineteenth-century France.

14   A curious inflection of this would be to consider cinema as part of a lineage that commences from the Middle Ages in Germany's *Narrtürmer*, passing into other European countries until, as Foucault

points out, at least 1815 in Britain (Foucault 1987: 68). This is the institutional displaying of the insane to the public, so that it was seen as mass spectacle: 'now it was madness itself, madness in flesh and blood, which was put on show' (Foucault 1987: 69). What is at issue for cinema is the ontology of the madness – how much different is a documentary that shows madness (as defined by psychiatry or the legal system) and a narrative film in terms of what the spectator and the culture does with the images? This is an issue for further discussion and something we shall return to at various times in the ensuing chapters. Further to this, cinema's relationship to madness borrows at least one aspect from the eighteenth century – the idea that madness is a site for spectacle.

15 The serial killer films of the 1980s and 90s – and quite possibly beyond this period – represent a curious return to many of the key themes and ideas of the classical period. Note, for example, how close the following passage – Foucault's description of the style and intent of the latter part of the eighteenth century – matches these film's depictions of not just the killers, but the social environs: 'The madness of desire, insane murders, the most unreasonable passions – all are wisdom and reason, since they are a part of the order of nature. Everything that morality and religion, everything that a clumsy society has stifled in man, revives in the castle of murders' (Foucault 1987: 282).

16 And later Foucault states: 'In classical confinement, the madman was also vulnerable to observation, but such observation did not, basically, involve him; it involved only his monstrous surface, his visible animality; and it included at least one form of reciprocity, since the sane man could read in the madman, as in a mirror, the imminent movement of his downfall' (Foucault 1987: 248). Here we find a moment where we observe this phenomenon represented in cinema as well as seeing in it part of the cinematic experience. In other words, we may well see such ideas of the observation of madness, the monstrous surface, and the parallels between the sane and madness as they are mirroring the other; and we can also see how cinema participates in this same process that originates from the eighteenth century. That is, part of cinema's function has become the observation, surfacing, imaging, and holding up of madness as a mirror.

17 This issue of mirrors and doubles will be taken up in a later section, but just to give some indication of what is in mind here the following examples may be useful: obsessions of reflexivity (the killer and his/her pursuer, Clarice Starling and Hannibal Lecter, John Doe and David Mills in *Se7en*); the obsession with reflections (*Single White Female*, Schroeder 1992); mirroring the past (*Psycho*, *Vertigo* – indeed Hitchcock's cinema is one of mirrors, with literal examples being found in almost all of the films).

18 We will return to this history of hysteria and the various explanations given to it through time in Chapter five.

19 The case study of Dora, which Freud always considered one that remained unfinished, became the site of interpretation and debate, not the least because of this aspect of power and powerlessness. Dora thus became both a symbol of power and resistance as well as one of psychoanalytic manipulation and restraint.

20 As Foucault points out: 'The scandal of unreason produced only the contagious example of transgression and immorality; the scandal of madness showed men how close to animality their Fall could bring them' (Foucault 1987: 81). This is the movement from the Renaissance sense of madness to the Classical and marks, for Foucault, a fundamental aspect of the relationship of madness to reason. This is the bond of one to the other.

21 Although not expressly concerned with madness, Edward Said's *Orientalism* illustrates well the West's attitude towards the non-European in these terms of difference. Compare his discussion of Delacroix's images of North Africa and the images of madness and bestiality.

22 'The theme of the animal-madman was effectively realised in the eighteenth century, in occasional attempts to impose a certain pedagogy on the insane. Pinel cites the case of a "very famous monastic establishment, in one of the southern regions of France," where a violent madman would be given "a precise order to change"' (Foucault 1987: 75).

23 For example: 'passion is no longer simply one of the causes – however powerful – of madness; rather it forms the basis for its very possibility. . . .The possibility of madness is therefore implicit in the very phenomenon of passion. . . . it saw that the *determinism of the passions* was nothing but a chance for madness to penetrate the world of reason. . . . Madness, made possible by passion, threatened by a movement proper to itself what had made passion itself possible' (Foucault 1987: 88; 89).

24 The *Scream* series is an obvious example. Even in films where there seems to be a defined other, such as the *Nightmare on Elm Street* series or the *I Know What You Did Last Summer* series, we often see incriminations and paranoia about others in the group.

25 Forgetting is perhaps one of the primary aspects of resistance that Freud speaks of in *The Interpretation of Dreams*. See also the Addenda to 'Inhibition, Symptom, Anxiety' (Freud 1987) for further discussion by Freud on resistances. Finally, a great deal of the material in the case studies can be read in terms of the struggle with resistance to analysis – see especially Freud's resignation to the resistance of Dora in the case study of that name. Dora becomes the embodiment of a resistance to analysis, and the fact that she terminates the sessions with Freud confirms for him her power to do this.

Chapter 3

26 How curious it is this similarity between the Rat Man's obsessions and those of Travis Bickle! Both have an obsession to protect a woman (who is seen by both men as a figure of love); both become obsessed by the condition of their bodies – the Rat Man to slim, Bickle to become fit to fight decay; both become obsessed with forms of language – the Rat Man would repeatedly say to people when they had spoken to him 'What was it you said just then?' (Freud 1990b: 70), and Bickle's diary, his jokes and word play, and the famous repetition of 'You talkin' to me?'. The political figure, Charles Palentine, that Betsy campaigns for can be read as a type of father figure to Bickle – first to be honoured and then to be killed in a version of the Oedipal drive to depose the father and assume his position.

27 This is a fairly common interplay in this type of film. Witness any number of films where the central theme is a hunt for a criminal and invariably the spectator shares knowledge from both perspectives, but, like the pursuers, less than the criminal him/herself. *Silence of the Lambs* is another obvious example.

28 This is the moment in the film when, for the first time, the rain seems to have stopped, there is daylight and sunshine. It is the first moment outside of the city, and the tightness of the urban spaces gives way to seemingly unending dusty plains. The control that John Doe has asserted for the entire film continues to be shown in this change of scenery. What is perhaps most interesting about the imagery of the final scenes in the film is that it works against any sense of a binary divide between culture and nature. What we are shown is not the natural, but an environment stripped bare by humanity.

29 The difficulty of the translation of *Angst* for anxiety urges a return to the original term. *Angst* functions in English now perhaps more readily since Freud, and seems more accurate than the various translations. Freud draws attention to the particular sense of *Angst* at various times, most directly when distinguishing between it, as a state, *Furcht* (fear), with its strong connection to the object, and *Schreck* (fright) which results from a lack of preparation. See, for example, Freud 1986: 443.

30 See especially Lacan's seminar *The Psychoses* for notes on this. Of course this is more than just the process of functioning, for the formation of the defence is used by psychoanalysis to read the neurosis. In other words, how the signs of the defence are interpreted will indicate the interpretation of the neurosis. For Lacan, this is part of the locating of the neurosis within the Symbolic by examining the attachment of the signifier to the signified.

31 It is worth recalling here that although the cinematic text is our primary example, the central points are equally applicable to other textual forms. Looking at a painting or reading a novel have different

textual systems to create such effects, but the spectator is engaging in a fundamentally common process.

32 Freud's examples of such displacements include the relinquishing of masturbatory phantasies for a real person, a woman giving up incestuous wishes for her father for marriage, a woman's phantasies of prostitution given up for monogamy. See Freud 1987 pp. 122–3.

33 See Lacan's *Seminar XX: Encore*, especially the final two sections entitled 'Rings of Strings' and 'The Rat in the Maze'.

34 This is an issue we shall take up in the final chapter, which is more directly concerned with the relationship between madness, knowledge and the role of cinema.

35 Another way of approaching this Hegelian model would be to think about the sense of truth in the making of the film as it is inserted into the act of spectating. For example, *Pixote* (Babenco 1981) uses real street children in Brazil. But even if they are homeless children (their truth) when filmed, do they still have that same status when the film is watched in ten or twenty years' time? This is not a question of whether such a child is an actual street child in Brazil, but the shift in the status of truth in that identity.

36 *Seminaire XX: Encore*, where this discussion takes place, was the seminar of 1972–3. There would only be another 5 after this. Roudinesco sees Lacan's obsessions as being tied to his aging: 'Dreading the signs of the old age that he knew would ultimately put an end to his intellectual activities and personal attractiveness, he was increasingly haunted by a fear of self-destruction that led him to reexamine the great myths on which he had based his interpretation of Freud: castration, residue, sex, *jouissance*, the letter, death, mysticism, and the trinity' (Roudinesco 1997: 358).

37 Which echoes, yet is distinct from, Lacan's other construction of the subject and knowledge – the analyst as *sujet supposé savoir*. This subject who is supposed to know is, for Lacan, constructed by the patient in the analytic situation. What is really taking place is the contesting of a knowledge which psychoanalysis itself admits cannot exist.

38 '*Le monde, le monde de l'être plein de savoir, ce n'est qu'un rêve*' (Lacan 1975: 114) (The world, the world of being and full of knowledge, is only a dream).

39 We must put to one side for the moment this important issue of psychosis. It will be dealt with in the following chapter.

Chapter 4

40 'The psychoses, if you like – there is no reason to deny oneself the luxury of this word – correspond to what has always been called and legitimately continues to be called *madness*' (Lacan 1993: 4).

41 It is too far beyond our direct concerns here, but it is easy to see the ways in which this interplay of any form of resistance can, or has, been positioned as a form of madness. The hegemonic structures, informing the ideologies of a cultural order, have used the sense of madness to alienate and disempower different forms of resistance. The supposed madness of the cultural other is to be seen in the representation of non-whites in colonial discourse (for example Delacroix's images of North Africans); the feminine as a madness against patriarchy; the madness of youth against the supposed wisdom of the elders. To label a perceived resistance as madness is one of the panoptic forces of control.

42 And here we can only indicate Wittgenstein's idea of *Sprachspiel* (language-game) – of the interplay between the recognition of the meaning of the utterance (or, in this case, image) and the need to be acquainted with the game itself. This is the contrasting and yet related game of reality, cinema and madness. This issue of meaning, and the representation of meaning, lies at the heart of this study.

43 Daniel Paul Schreber was an articulate and well-known lawyer. He ran for election (and lost) in 1884 and shortly after began to suffer mental troubles. He was treated by Paul Flechsig, spending lengthy periods in hospital. In 1903 he published his *Memoirs of My Mental Illness*, which is an extraordinary account of his delusions, written in a style that becomes almost convincing at times. Freud was fascinated by these writings and wrote a case study based on them.

Pierre Rivière was a semi-literate French peasant who, in 1835, murdered his mother, his eighteen-year-old sister and seven-year-old brother. Whilst in jail he wrote a memoir to explain why he had acted this way.

44 This sacrifice is mentioned many times by Rivière, and often carries with it a comparison to Christ: 'The latest book I read was a history of shipwrecks lent to me by Lerot. I found in it that when the sailors lacked victuals, they sacrificed one of the their number and ate him to save the rest of the crew. I thought to myself: I too will sacrifice myself for my father, everything seemed to invite me to this deed' (Foucault 1982: 106).

45 To quote two examples of many: 'But for us to have a psychosis there must be disturbances of language' and 'We must insist upon the presence of these disorders [of language] before making a diagnosis of psychosis' (Lacan 1993: 92).

46 Paranoid psychosis is read here in both the sense of a psychosis derived from paranoid feelings, and acts of paranoia originating from an underlying psychosis.

47 Lacan translates Freud's *Verwerfung* as *retranchement*, which has connotations of cutting off, stopping the supply of something, as well as a militaristic sense of digging in (and so an act of defence). He also offers *forclusion* (foreclosure).

48 For the discussion of fetishism in these terms of disavowal see Freud's essay 'Fetishism'.

49 Significantly, even in the extremes of psychosis Lacan sees not a necessary collapse of discourse in terms of the Symbolic order: 'A delusion is not necessarily unrelated to Normal discourse and the subject is well able to convey it to us, to his own satisfaction, within a world in which communication is not entirely broken off' (Lacan 1993: 88).

50 The theories I have in mind here would include: Barthes' ideas on the birth of the reader, of texts of *jouissance* (in, for example, *The Pleasure of the Text* (1980) and 'From Work to Text'), the operation of the *punctum* as discussed in *Camera Lucida*; Ingarden, Iser and Ruthrof and the phenomenological idea of the reader; Eco's semiotic interpretation of the act of reading in *Theory of Semiotics* (1976); even Foucault's questioning of the status of the author in 'What is an Author?' would be part of this composition.

51 And this is true of even a relatively sophisticated reading of identification such as the one that Metz offers.

52 'From the moment the subject speaks, the Other, with a big O, is there. Without this there would be no problem of psychosis. Psychotics would be speaking machines' (Lacan 1993: 41).

53 Interestingly, Lacan actually terms this the specular other of the ego in the Seminar of the previous year to the one on psychoses (see Lacan 1988b pp. 243–4). Lacan's specular other of the ego works in terms of the Imaginary, that is self-reflexivity, and for here we see this as the image relation that is required in order to become a spectator.

54 Rycroft discusses how one of his patients – a schizophrenic – reveals how the literal madness can operate in such a spectator: 'His rare visits to the cinema led him to make comments which clearly showed his inability to distinguish what kind of experience he was having. After seeing a humorous film in which Danny Kaye falls in love with his beautiful young female psychoanalyst, his only comment was surprise that such a young and attractive woman should have been allowed to practice'. (Rycroft 1968: 87).

55 This also takes us back to the earlier discussion on the subject, the ego, and the Other. Lacan argues that it is the role of the ideal-ego as a 'strange twin' of the ego in the formation of phantasy and psychosis (Lacan 1993: 144).

56 Lacan's comments on repression are particularly relevant to the discussion at hand, and it is useful to quote in greater length this passage. The insertions provide indications to the analysis of film: 'Each symbolic chain we are linked to comprises an internal coherence [the filmic narrative] ... Now, it sometimes happens that we are unable to do this on all levels at once – in other words, we find the law intolerable [the 'as if' phenomenon]. Not that it is intolerable in itself, but the position we are in comprises a sacrifice that proves to be

impossible at the level of meaning [the spectator refuses the narrative sequence as having coherent meaning]. So we repress some of our own acts, discourse, or behavior [the act of spectating can continue]. But the chain nevertheless continues to run on beneath the surface, express its demands, and assert its claims – and this it does through the intermediary of the neurotic symptom [cinema and the act of spectating]' (Lacan 1993: 84).

Chapter 5

57 Charcot, the flamboyant French neurologist who had such a profound impact on the young Freud, would demonstrate his 'cures' on patients in front of a packed audience of doctors and scientists. This often involved dramatic performances where the body of the hysteric would contort and swoon in the presence of Charcot.

58 The Good, like other capitalisations here (such as the Law), are used to denote an institution or as a conceptual demarcation to distinguish it from the 'good'. There is perhaps the danger of a Platonic ideal here, but what is really intended is a sense of the Good as an unrealised definitional concept, and the good as particular manifestations. This is not dissimilar to Lacan's ideas of the Other and the *objet petit a*.

59 Lacan returns to the interplay between Kant and Sade often, but of particular note in these terms are the piece 'Kant *avec* Sade' and in the discussions in *The Ethics of Psychoanalysis*. For Foucault there is a sense of rupture in this philosophical alliance of Kant and Sade. For him it is a fundamental part of our contemporary culture's attitude towards the transgressive: 'How is it possible to discover, under all these different figures, that form of thought we carelessly call' 'the philosophy of eroticism,' but in which it would be necessary to recognize (which is no less, but also much more) an essential experience for our culture since Kant and Sade – the experience of finitude and being, of the limit and transgression? What is the proper space of the form of thought and what language can't it adopt? (Foucault 2000: 77). In many ways this is the struggle of cinema as madness as it attempts to create the space both within and for the spectator.

60 The most obvious example in film is the star system. The goods (products) of beauty find their manifestation in the bodies, faces, voices of the stars of the day.

61 And, as further illustration, Kant elsewhere states: 'In presenting the sublime in nature the mind feels *agitated*, while in an aesthetic judgement about the beautiful in nature it is in *restful* contemplation' (Kant 1987: 258).

62 For more on this see Freud's various writings on civilisation and constructions of morality. Of particular interest is ' "Civilised" Sexual

Morality and Modern Nervous Illness', as well as the extended piece 'Group Psychology and the Analysis of the Ego' (Freud 1987).

63 I have discussed this elsewhere in relation to film. See Fuery (2000) *New Developments in Film Theory*.

64 Lacan argues that the fragmented sense of self is partly formed through the actions of alienation (from the objects of desire) and aphanisis (a fear of the loss of the signifier of the self). For further discussion of this see Lacan (1986) *The Four Fundamental Concepts of Psychoanalysis*.

65 Whether or not Derrida is conscious of it, this theme of his temporary disfigurement returns in different guises throughout his *Memoirs of the Blind*. There are constant returns to this idea of fear, loss and looking, in particular of the gaze at the self.

66 Compare this to the shifting status of Angela in *American Beauty* as she moves from the impossible beauty not to be touched, lying in the fantasm of roses (with the contradictory status – for Lester – as sexually active), to the nervous virginal teenager who reveals her true (sexual) identity.

67 The ideal ego, according to Freud, is that which the ego perceives as that which 'observes, criticizes and compares, and in that way sets itself over against the other part of the ego' (Freud 1986: 479). In this way, it is both a part of and a part from the sense of the self.

Chapter 6

68 This is retold by Foucault in his essay 'Nietzsche, Freud, Marx'. The German for superego is of course *das Über-Ich*. It is also interesting to recall that Freud always insisted that one of the primary sources of the prohibitive nature/sense of the superego was from reading, and not the figure of the parent (a more obvious source). It would be useful to trace this line in terms of the function of cinema as part of the superego process.

69 In different ways the sorts of models developed by Foucault in, for example, *The Archaeology of Knowledge* (1972) and *The Order of Things* (1970) and Thomas Kuhn's *The Structure of Scientific Revolution*, with its theory of paradigm shifts, demonstrate this process. What causes shifts in knowledge and interpretation is a complex interconnection of a whole series of events rather than a single idea, even if it is the idea that becomes distilled and the focus of attention.

70 There is more, much more, we can gather from someone like Wittgenstein here. However, just a single quote is all that will be allowed or else we run the danger of transgressing our own project. Wittgenstein speaks of the dream image in a way that proves useful to this issue of knowledge and cinema: 'It can certainly be said that contemplation of the dream-image inspires us, that we just *are*

inspired. Because if we tell someone else our dream the image will not usually inspire him. The dream affects us as does an idea pregnant with possible developments' (Wittgenstein 1978: 69). This is the line of becoming a spectator – the film can inspire this spectator, whilst leaving another cold. Thus madness in one, calmness in the other.

71 For example: 'At the level of discourses and their domains, however, practically the opposite phenomenon occurred. There was a steady proliferation of discourses concerned with sex – specific discourses, different from one another both by their form and by their object: a discursive ferment that gathered momentum from the eighteenth century onward. ... But more important was the multiplication of discourses concerning sex in the field of exercise of power itself: an institutional incitement to speak about it, and to do so more and more; a determination on the part of the agencies of power to hear it spoken about, and to cause *it* to speak through explicit articulation and endlessly accumulated detail' (Foucault 1984: 18).

72 Here we see one of the recurring motifs and representational fields of madness and homosexuality in films. Many films will use dislocated images of lesbianism, for example, to show the madness of a situation. By this, we have in mind the countless images in films of the 'normal' and rational character finding themselves in a carnivalesque world populated by strangely dressed people (often with hints of drug taking) with flashes of women kissing. Such a kiss does not stand for lesbianism however, but for the forbidden, otherness of the situation. Similarly, a common representation of gay men has been the alternative, otherness to the normal world of people. Where, one must ask, is the ordinariness of gay life?

73 We have referred to this elsewhere. It is Lacan's 'formula' of desire and otherness – the objects of a little otherness (*autre*).

74 Which in itself is a curious idea – is the production of loss still production? If loss is the result can we still speak of production?

75 S◇a is Lacan's symbol for phantasy. It is the split subject caught up in an almost contradictory relationship of alienation and complete seduction for those objects of desire. See, for example, his discussion of alienation and aphanisis in *The Four Fundamental Concepts of Psychoanalysis*.

76 For example: 'All love is based on a certain relationship between two unconscious knowledges' (Lacan 1998: 144). There is always a form of love involved in the spectator's relationship to cinema – we love the image, we feign falling in love with the characters and events, love is a topic of so much cinema, and so on.

77 This care is related to the Heideggerian *cura* (care) which, via Kristeva, we read as: '*Care* thus becomes the "basis on which *every* interpretation of *Dasein* which is ontical and belongs to a world view must move" ... As a result, care constitutes the primordial mortar in

the phenomenological edifice and its structural *articulation*, its impetus or ferment, and the logic governing its development and structure' (Kristeva 1984:128). This status of care forms part of the status of what it is to be a spectator.

78 The term signifier here – and elsewhere throughout this discussion – is used in the sense given to it by Lacan. It has a meaning effect (*effet de signifié*) (Lacan 1998: 18) and so carries with it the sense of meaning something, even if what that something is is not known or cannot even be known.

79 The context in which Derrida is speaking is the philosophical one: 'In the context of our discussion, this affects the whole philosophical history of analysis, from the royal weaver of the Platonic dialectic to the dialectic of the Hegelian presupposition, from the topics and analytics of Aristotle to Kant's transcendental analytic and the reckoning with *a priori* synthetic judgement' (Derrida 1998: 19). Such a sense of resistance runs counter to the philosophical analysis that 'work toward the lifting of such resistances' (Derrida 1998: 19). Furthermore, this is part of a larger order of resistance that became, for Freud, one of the key aspects of psychoanalytic theory, and for Derrida part of the issue of philosophical analysis. This is 'a "resistance to analyse" that figures *both* the most resistant resistance, resistance par excellence, hyperbolic resistance, *and* the one that disorganizes the very principle, the constitutive idea of psychoanalysis as analysis of resistances' (Derrida 1998: 22). This, we argue here, is part of cinema as madness.

80 A simple example of this can be drawn from one of the well-known surrealist films. The famous scene in *Un chien andalou* where the ants emerge out of the hand of the man would seem resistant to meaning, full of nightmarish qualities and inexplicable causes. However, there is part of this image which relates to the French saying for the sensation of pins and needles – *Avoir des fourmis dans la main*. However just because this seems to explain the image, it does not really resolve the meaning of such an image within the film.

81 Consider further the idea that when we become the spectator of a film how much of the reality of that film subsumes us. This is one of the primary characteristics of the psychotic, and a version of its operation is to be found in the spectator. So Lacan's description of the relationship of reality and the psychotic can also be seen in terms of the spectator. This idea finds its parallel in cinema: a reality (film) structured (conventions of cinema and spectatorship) by the presence of a particular signifier (filmic signifiers as they create a form of reality through the act of spectating).

Bibliography

Barthes, Roland *The Pleasure of the Text*, trans. R. Miller, New York: Hill and Wang, 1980.

—— *Camera Lucida*, trans. R. Howard, London: Flamingo, 1984.

—— *Lover's Discourse: Fragments*, trans. R. Howard, Middlesex: Penguin, 1990.

Bateson, Gregory *Steps to an Ecology of Mind*, London: Paladin,1978.

Derrida, Jacques *Disseminations*, trans. B. Johnson, London: Athlone Press, 1981.

—— *Memoirs of the Blind*, trans. P. A. Brault and M. Naas, Chicago: University of Chicago Press, 1990.

—— 'Sending: On Representation' in P. Fuery, ed., *Representation, Discourse and Desire*, Melbourne: Longman, 1994, pp. 9–34.

—— *Resistances of Psychoanalysis*, trans. Peggy Kamuf, Pascale-Anne Brault, and Michael Naas, Stanford: Stanford University Press, 1998.

Eco, Umberto *A Theory of Semiotics*, Bloomington: Indiana University Press, 1976.

Foucault, Michel *The Order of Things*, London: Tavistock, 1970.

—— *Archaeology of Knowledge*, trans. A. Sheridan-Smith, London: Tavistock, 1972.

—— *Histoire de la Folie*, Paris: Gallimard, 1972.

—— *I, Pierre Rivière, having slaughtered my mother, my sister, and my brother. . .* trans. Frank Jellinek, Lincoln and London: University of Nebraska Press, 1975.

—— 'Interview with Michel Foucault', in H. Dreyfus and P. Rabinow, *Michel Foucault: Beyond Structuralism and Hermeneutics*, Chicago: University of Chicago Press, 1983.

—— *History of Sexuality, Vol. 1*, trans. R. Hurley, New York: Vintage Books, 1984.

—— *Madness and Civilization: A History of Insanity in the Age of Reason*, trans. R. Howard, London: Tavistock, 1987.

—— *Aesthetics: Essential Works of Foucault 1954–1984*, ed., James D. Faubion, London: Penguin, 2000.

Freud, Sigmund *New Introductory Lectures on Psychoanalysis*, trans. J. Strachey, London: Hogarth Press, 1964.

—— *Jokes and Their Relation to the Unconscious*, trans. J. Strachey, Middlesex: Penguin, 1983.

—— *The Interpretation of Dreams*, trans. J, Strachey, Middlesex: Penguin, 1985.

—— *On Psychoanalysis*, trans. J. Strachey, Middlesex: Penguin, 1987.

—— *Introductory Lectures on Psychoanalysis*, trans. J. Strachey, Middlesex: Penguin, 1986.

—— *Art and Literature*, trans. J. Strachey, Middlesex: Penguin, 1990a.

—— *Case Histories II*, trans. J. Strachey, Middlesex: Penguin, 1990b.

—— *Civilization, Society and Religion*, J. Strachey, Middlesex: Penguin, 1991.

Fuery, Patrick *New Developments in Film Theory*, Palgrave/Macmillan: London: 2000.

Hegel, G.W.F. *Phenomenology of Spirit*, trans. A. V. Miller, Oxford: Oxford University Press, 1977.

Iser, Wolfgang *The Act of Reading*, Indianapolis: Indiana University Press, 1978.

Kant, Immanuel *Critique of Pure Reason*, trans. Norman Kemp Smith, New York: St. Martin's Press, 1987.

Klein, Melanie *Love, Guilt, and Reparation and Other Essays*, London: Virago, 1988.

Kojève, Alexandre *Introduction to the Reading of Hegel*, trans. James H. Nichols, Jr., Ithaca and London: Cornell University Press, 1980.

Kristeva, Julia *Revolution in Poetic Language*, trans. M. Waller, New York: Columbia University Press, 1984.

Kuhn, Thomas *The Structure of Scientific Revolutions*, Chicago: University of Chicago Press, 1974.

Lacan, Jacques *Encore*, Éditions du Seuil, Paris: 1975.

—— *The Four Fundamental Concepts of Psychoanalysis*, trans. A. Sheridan, Middlesex: Penguin, 1986.

—— *Freud's Papers on Technique*, trans. J. Forrester, ed. J.-A. Miller, Cambridge: Cambridge University Press, 1988a.

—— *The Ego in Freud's Theory and in the Technique of Psychoanalysis*, trans. S Tomaselli, ed., J.-A. Miller, Cambridge: Cambridge University Press, 1988b.

—— *L'Envers de la psychanalyse*, Paris: Editions du Seuil, 1991.

—— *The Ethics of Psychoanalysis*, trans. D. Porter, ed. J.-A. Miller, London: Routledge, 1992.

—— *The Psychoses*, trans. R. Grigg, ed., J.-A. Miller, London: Routledge, 1993.

—— *Encore*, trans. B. Fink New York: Norton, 1998.

Matlock, Jan *Scenes of Seduction*, New York: Columbia University Press, 1994.

Roudinesco, Elizabeth *Jacques Lacan*, trans. B. Bray, London: Polity Press, 1997.

Rycroft, Charles *Imagination and Reality*, London: Hogarth Press, 1968.

Wittgenstein, Ludwig *Culture and Value*, trans. Peter Winch, ed., G. H. von Wright, Oxford: Blackwell, 1978.

Index